Pray to Live

Pray to Live

Thomas Merton: A Contemplative Critic

Henri J. M. Nouwen

FIDES PUBLISHERS, INC.
NOTRE DAME, INDIANA

Translated from the Dutch by DAVID SCHLAVER, C.S.C.

Nouwen, Henri J.   M
    Pray to live.

    Translation of Bidden om het leven.
    Includes texts by T. Merton.
    Bibliography: p. 153
    1. Merton, Thomas, 1915-1968. I. Merton, Thomas,
1915-1968. II. Title.
BX4705.M542N6813   255′.125′024 [B]   72-10395
ISBN 0-8190-0580-0

To Richard Alan White

Preface

More than three years have now passed since the death of Thomas Merton (Father Louis, as we knew him at Gethsemani). There have been a number of writings since he died which attempt to evaluate his life and work, some of them very useful and providing insight into one aspect or other of his personality or writings, others quite misleading.

It will require a considerable period of time before there can be any adequate attempt to present Merton's life and work in its true context and to evaluate its meaning and significance for our times. This has always been true of men whose personality and energy have been striking enough to mark a significant part of their world with their own unique stamp. The full meaning of a man's life and the breadth of his character appear only with the flow of time when the seeds of new and hidden forms of life planted by his hand have been able to appear and flower. In the case of Thomas Merton the sheer mass of his writings poses formidable problems to anyone who would attempt to present his thought to the world. The fact that only a small fraction of the fifteen journals he wrote have been published and only a few of the several thousands of letters—some of them veritable treatises, and all of them containing important information for understanding his rich and complex personality—makes it impossible to achieve anything like a definitive portrait of the man or sketch of his thought at this time.

Still there is a very great deal of material available already and Henri Nouwen has made broad and judicious use of it. He has touched the heart of Merton's writings, sought out the source of his inspiration and energy and displayed the connections between the various articulations of this vision of truth. He has seen that for Merton the way to relevance was the way of prayer and contemplation. The source of Thomas Merton's social and political critique was not based on public debate and analysis but rather on a contemplative penetration into the heart of God where he discovered the concrete man living on earth today. Merton himself brought all his own experience, his sins and sufferings, but also his sensitivity for beauty and truth, to this contemplative discovery. He came to feel the plight of every man who knew suffering, especially suffering inflicted by his fellow man. And he felt it with passion of profound identification. No one more than Merton showed that the monastic life is not a retreat from

reality. On the contrary, his social and political critique was the fruit of a compassion learned through a
life of monastic ascesis and contemplation.

Henri Nouwen met Merton but once. Yet, by a sympathy of feeling and perception he has understood the
central motivating force of Merton's life: meditation
and prayer. He has seen this more truly and profoundly
than some who, while claiming to be intimate friends
of Merton, have altogether missed the point of his work
and life through lack of feeling for his vision of God,
man and the cosmos. There is nothing surprising in this
fact. True understanding depends not only on intelligence and proximity but above all on the heart.

Some of us had the chance to know Thomas Merton
for a long time, day by day, as brothers know one another: simply, immediately and unpretentiously. Some
of us knew him too as a disciple knows his master, as a
student knows his teacher and as a doctor knows his
patient. We knew him in good days and bad, at his best
and at his worst. We loved him as a brother, for he was
a most lovable man in his unfailing and unpretentious
accessibility. But above all we valued him as a man of
God, with an unfailing and boundless enthusiasm for
the monastic life and for the practices that were most
central to contemplation, especially silence and solitude. We came to see that when he spoke with compassion for the oppressed of the earth that itself was
being defiled and polluted by man, he spoke out of an
awareness bought with his own anguish of heart and
won by contemplative effort and insight. We saw that

he was compassionate because he knew himself as having received the compassion of God. And, finally, we saw that it was not so much his brilliant intelligence that gave him ready insight into sociological and political problems but rather his compassion.

Whatever may be said about Merton, if it will be said truly it must present his vision and his work as the fruit of the knowledge of God bought with a faith come alive through contemplation. Restoration of right order and peace in the world was for Merton the fruit of the vision of God arrived at through deep prayer. Henri Nouwen has seen Merton in this perspective and his book clearly reveals some of the concrete, practical consequences of this way of experiencing life. In reading this book one can meet, for a brief moment, the living spirit of Merton. It is a refreshing encounter.

John Eudes Bamberger O.C.S.O.
Abbot of the Genesee

Contents

Introduction

This book is meant to be an introduction to the life and thought of Thomas Merton. I met him only once, at the Abbey of Our Lady of Gethsemani in Kentucky. Yet thereafter, his person and work had such an impact on me, that his sudden death stirred me as if it were the death of one of my closest friends. It therefore seems natural for me to write for others about the man who has inspired me most in recent years.

I have tried here to uncover a few main trends in Merton's richly diverse and very productive life, in order to help in a better understanding of his commitment to a contemplative critique of himself and his world. I hope that these short chapters will lead to an attentive meditation of Merton's own writings and to a continuing search for a contemplative foundation of our fragmented, restless lives.

Therefore I have divided this book in two parts. The first part ("For Instruction") can be seen as a preparation for a lively reflection on the second part ("For Meditation") which contains exclusively short excerpts of Merton's own works.

I am very grateful to David Schlaver, Joe Freeman, Steve Thomas and Barbara Henry for their generous help in the preparation of the manuscript and to Inday Day for her competent secretarial assistance.

Special thanks I owe to John Eudes Bamberger, abbot of the Genesee, who for many years shared Merton's life as a monk at Gethsemani Abbey in Kentucky and knew him well not only as his personal friend but also as his physician. His willingness to annotate the text and to write the preface made me overcome my hesitation to publish this book.

I have dedicated this book to Richard Alan White. His strong friendship and penetrating criticisms of my ideas and life style gave me a deeper appreciation of Merton's intuition that contemplation and revolution are two forms of radicalism which never should be separated.

Part I

FOR INSTRUCTION

List of Abbreviations

A Short Biography

Thomas Merton was born on January 31, 1915 in Prades, France. His father was a painter, a New Zealander by birth; his mother, who also painted, originally came from Ohio. He was the older of two boys (John Paul, born in 1918, was killed in 1943 during an air battle over the English channel). Although Thomas' father seldom or never visited a church and his mother only now and then went to Quaker meetings, he was still baptized. This apparently had few consequences for his upbringing.

In 1916 the Merton family moved to the United States and went to live on Long Island. When Thomas was six his mother died and he and his brother went to live with their grandparents, while his father, as before, continued to make trips to exhibit his canvases. In 1925 the elder Merton took his son with him to France and sent him to study in the lyceum in Montauban. In his fourteenth year Thomas went with his father to England and there entered high school in Oakham (Rutland). Already during this period he was developing a great interest in English literature; William Blake, D. H. Lawrence and James Joyce were his favorite authors.

In 1931, Thomas' father died in London from a brain tumor. Thomas, then sixteen, finished his studies in Oakham, and received a scholarship for Clare College in Cambridge. But in 1933, he returned to the United States where again he lived with his grandparents. During his vacations, he had traveled throughout Europe, especially in Italy and Germany where he gathered the impressions which he used in his first novel. In 1935, at the age of twenty, he went to Columbia University and studied Spanish, German, geology, constitutional law and French literature. There he joined the communist youth movement and became art editor for the student publication *Jester*.

Through the book, *The Spirit of Medieval Philosophy*, by Etienne Gilson, Thomas Merton became interested in scholasticism. He followed the courses on St. Thomas and Dun Scotus given by Daniel Walsh who later became a friend of his. In these years he also developed a close friendship with Bramachari, a Buddhist monk who pointed him toward the great riches of Christendom. In 1938 he undertook religion lessons with Father Moore, who received him into the Catholic Church on November 16th of that year.

At twenty-four, upon receiving his master's degree in English literature at Columbia, he became an English teacher at the City College of New York and a reporter for the *New York Times* and the *New York Herald Tribune*. Through many conversations with his friend Bob Lax and by studying St. John of the Cross, he began to feel a desire to become a priest.

At first he wanted to become a Franciscan, but when it was made clear to him in a discourteous manner that he didn't have a vocation, he dropped this plan.

From 1939 to 1941 he taught English at St. Bonaventure's College in New York. During his two years there Thomas Merton led an almost monastic life, wrote a diary, three novels—none of which was accepted for publication—and went on retreat at the Trappist monastery in Gethsemani, Kentucky. In 1941 Merton left St. Bonaventure's and went to work in the black ghetto of Harlem under the direction of Baroness Catherine de Hueck.

After a second visit to the Trappists of Gethsemani, he decided to join them. He gave his clothes to the blacks in Harlem, his books to the Franciscans and a friend, tore up two of his novels and sent the rest—his poetry, a manuscript of the novel "Journal of my Escape from the Nazis," and his diary—to his friend Mark Van Doren.

Completely alone, with a small dufflebag in his hand, twenty-six year old Thomas Merton arrived at Gethsemani on December 10, 1942. He remained there until 1965 as member of the community, and until 1968 as a hermit. The publication of his autobiography *The Seven Storey Mountain* in 1948 made Merton suddenly an internationally known author, whose many books and articles deepened the spiritual life of many Christians and non-Christians throughout the world. In the twenty-six years of his Trappist life he left the cloister only on a few occasions. When he was fifty-three, in 1968, he received permission to make an orientation trip to the Far East. In attending this conference of abbots from Christian contemplative monasteries in Asia, he had hoped to become more intimate with Eastern spirituality. He visited many Buddhist monasteries, spoke on various occasions with the Dalai Lama, led discussions and gave a lecture for the monks and nuns who had gathered for the conference.

On December 10, 1968, shortly after his lecture, he was found dead in his room. Contact with a defectively wired fan had electrocuted him. His body was brought back to his monastery and on December 17 he was buried at Gethsemani.

CHAPTER 1

From Sarcasm to Contemplation

Today we know Thomas Merton as one of the most impressive contemplatives of our time. Yet in his youth, we find him more a sardonic and witty spectator, in whom the seeds of contemplation only gradually come to fruition. Even more than his detailed autobiography *The Seven Storey Mountain,* which Thomas Merton wrote in Gethsemani, his diary *The Secular Journal* unveils for us the life of the young Merton. In this diary, written long before it was published, we find the direct, spontaneous reactions of a young intellectual who does not yet know whether the world is to be loved or ridiculed.

The short, fragmentary diary lets us see Thomas Merton as an intelligent, well-read and well-traveled "graduate," who with poignant sarcasm perceives his surroundings and gives his commentary on them. Most noticeable in the *Journal,* perhaps, is the somewhat brutal nonchalance with which he criticizes the "stage" of the world. Nevertheless, by reading it we quickly recognize its writer to be an exceptionally sensitive young man, one who—parentless since his sixteenth year—was constantly searching, through travel and books, for something or someone to whom he could give his full dedication.

When Merton, almost twenty years after writing this diary, prepared the foreword for its publication, he said:

> Certainly the views and aspirations expressed, at times, with such dogmatic severity, have come to be softened and tempered with the passage of time and with a more intimate contact with the spiritual problems of other people. I hope I may be forgiven for having allowed some of my youthful sarcasms to survive in these pages. (*SJ*, p. 8)

It is perhaps good that he did not scrap this sarcasm, because it gives us possibly the best introduction to his contemplative spirit. We find a delightful example of Merton's view of his surroundings in his ironic description of the reaction of museum visitors to a painting by Brueghel. He writes:

> But what were the people saying about this picture? Two girls, art students probably: "It looks like one of the early French Impressionists." One Killer-of-a-Fellow, with a mob of female admirers: "Excellent reporting: look at those knees." (The knees were very knobby.)

One of two girls (giggling): "Look at them kissing, there."

A man: "That one's drunk, I guess."

Another Killer: "You can tell it's a Dutch painting: not a skinny one in the whole bunch."

A man (foreign accent): "Country dance!"

A woman: "Look at those white aprons."

A man: "Some paunch!"

A man: "Look at the pipers."

There were a lot of people who just read off the name, "Broo-gul," and walked on unabashed. But at least they must have thought it important. They came across with the usual reaction of people who don't know pictures are there to be enjoyed, but think they are things that have to be learned by heart to impress the bourgeoisie: so they tried to remember the name. (*SJ*, p. 29)

That is the young Merton. With a distant grin he observes his fellow men and women around him. Sarcasm gets the better of him.

But this early sarcasm is certainly not implacable cynicism, for it can quite easily turn into violent indignation. In the room with the painting of El Greco he heard a woman say: "They're all dying of TB," and he wrote:

Of course there were plenty of comments on the misery and unhappiness of the age the painter lived in. What would be the good of turning around and asking the old lady: "If the world was dying then, what do you suppose it is doing now, in this age of hypochondriacs and murderers and sterilizers? How about *our* pictures, are they dying of anything? Or can they be said to die, when they can't even come to life in order to do so?" (*SJ*, p. 30)

Merton wrote this when he was twenty-three. Five years later he was a Trappist and today he is rightly described as one of the most important spiritual writers of our century. It is surely true that the distant perception which appears in this diary has two sides. Distant perception leads to razor-sharp observation, which can lead to cynicism and bitterness; but it also can give rise to generous contemplation which is the source of real care and human concern.

Conversion and purification here were still to come. But in the progress recorded in this diary, we see a deep earnestness, which in the beginning is still somewhat hidden, come more and more to the foreground. The first pages are filled mostly with critical commentary on the books that he had read, the paintings that he had seen and the philosophies that inspired him. The gospel serves more to preserve all this at a certain playful distance than to let him feel deeply involved in his world. He wrote on William Blake, Dante, James Joyce, and Graham Greene, on Fra Angelico, Brueghel and El Greco, on St. Thomas and St. Augustine with a pointedness but also with the somewhat free-wheeling ease of a snobbish student. Scarcely two years a Catholic, he observed the world through the eyes of an enthusiastic but still naive convert.

Thus he traveled to Cuba where he glorified in rich poetical terms the life of Havana and made a fiery plea

for the genuineness of the Spanish religiosity in contrast to the superficiality of the American thought. His
Cuban diary perhaps belongs with the best prose that
he ever wrote.

Back in New York, his journal tells us he busied
himself again with writers, painters and philosophers,
until on April 7, 1941, on a trip to Gethsemani he wrote:
"I should tear out all the other pages of this book, and
all the other pages of anything else I have ever written
and begin here." (*SJ*, p. 155) That sounds like the cry
of a man who suddenly sees himself and his world in
their true form. As if unmasking his ironic distance and
discovering it to be vanity, he wrote: "I wonder if I
have learned enough to pray for humility. I desire only
one thing: to love God . . . to follow his will. . . . Could
it ever possibly mean that I might some day become a
monk in this monastery?" (*SJ*, p. 172)

The impact of this new experience was profound.
Back in New York he seemed to have lost orientation.
He mocked his interest in literature:

> I am amazed at all the novels I read between the ages of
> seventeen and twenty. . . . D. H. Lawrence, Stella Benson,
> Virginia Woolf, John Dos Passos, Jules Romains, Heming-
> way, Balzac, Flaubert, Celine. . . . I have read enough
> novels, and I don't want to read any more. Also, I think
> the novel is a lousy art form anyway. (*SJ*, p. 183)

The people around him became riddles to him. He
didn't speak of them anymore with a mocking smile,
but in despairing ignorance. "I have never been more

convinced than now that I see absolutely no sense in what people do." (*SJ*, p. 16) His novel *My Argument with the Gestapo,* which he wrote in the summer of 1941 after his visit to the Trappists, is like a long litany, with the refrain: I can't understand them: the soldiers who fight, the sailors who drown, the Germans who attack, the English who defend, the people who busy themselves, I cannot understand them. What is the sense in what people do? (See *MA*, p. 55-56)

In between he worked and lived at St. Bonaventure's College but constantly questioned himself as to whether this kind of teaching was the way he wanted to follow Christ. He felt the contradiction between the rich St. Patrick's Cathedral on Fifth Avenue and the poor black children of Harlem. He went there to work, but distrusted his motives. Wasn't this a compromise? Wasn't something more being demanded of him? Harlem or the Trappists? The choice preoccupied him but didn't make him anxious. He laughed at his busy past and wrote:

> No more excitements, arguments, tearing of hair, trips to Cuba and grandiose "farewell world" gestures. . . . Everything is indifferent except prayer, fasting, meditation—and work. (*SJ*, p. 216)

Still, his work in Harlem, did not keep his thoughts about Gethsemani from haunting him.

On November 27, 1941 he wrote:

> Why doesn't this idea of the Trappists leave me?. . . . But perhaps what I am afraid of is to write and be re-

jected. . . . Perhaps I cling to my independence, to the chance to write, to go where I like in the world. . . . It seems monstrous at the moment that I should consider my writing important enough even to enter the question. If God wants me to write, I can write anywhere. . . . But going to the Trappists is exciting, it fills me with awe and desire. I return to the idea again and again: "Give up *everything!*" (*SJ*, pp. 222-223)

With these words *The Secular Journal* closes, and with them, the life of the young Merton. Two weeks later he reported to Gethsemani to begin a spiritual journey—whose intensity and fascination make the many other journeys described in *The Seven Storey Mountain* seem like child's play.

CHAPTER 2

The Way to Silence

Once inside the walls of the Trappist abbey in Kentucky, Merton undertook a difficult path. Yet besides what we have discussed in the first chapter, there were various signs which brought him there. These were books, people and events—books, people and events, all of which made an impression on a young man, born of very artistic parents, already many years an orphan, constantly traveling between France, England and the United States. It is not surprising that we are dealing here with a man who sought. He sought a place where he could feel at home, he sought an insight by which to bring order to the endless series of opposing ideas which poured over him in his various schools, and he sought after beauty which could give him the satisfaction he had fleetingly found in the many things which were presented to him as art.

The influence of the books, people and events which brought Thomas Merton to Gethsemani can only be understood if we keep in mind his intense personality, which registered with a maximum sensitivity everything that he read, saw and experienced, always posing the question as large as life itself: "What can I say 'yes' to, without reserve?"

BOOKS

When Thomas Merton entered Columbia University in 1935, he was already very well read. In the London milieu, to which his godfather had introduced him, Hemingway, Joyce, D. H. Lawrence, Evelyn Waugh and Celine had become very familiar names to him. But there are two books especially which brought him to a deeper level of knowledge than the London literary circle: *The Spirit of Medieval Philosophy* by Etienne Gilson, and *Ends and Means* by Aldous Huxley.

With a sense of humor, Merton told how thankful he was that he hadn't thrown Gilson's book out the train window when he discovered to his great surprise the "Nihil obstat—imprimatur," and became conscious, to the point of aversion, that it was a Roman Catholic book.

From Gilson, Merton learned of the concept *aseitas*. Merton wrote:

In this one word, which can be applied to God alone, and which expresses His most characteristic attribute, I discovered an entirely new concept of God—a concept which showed me at once that the belief of Catholics was by no means the vague and rather superstitious hangover from an unscientific age that I had believed it to be. On the contrary, here was a notion of God that was at the same time deep, precise, simple and accurate and, what is more, charged with implications which I could not even begin to appreciate, but which I could at least dimly estimate, even with my own lack of philosophical training. (*SSM*, p. 172)

Aldous Huxley, who was one of Merton's favorite novelists, through his book, *Ends and Means*, was the first to bring him into contact with mysticism. Merton says about Huxley:

. . He had read widely and deeply and intelligently in all kinds of Christian and Oriental mystical literature, and had come out with the astonishing truth that all this, far from being a mixture of dreams and magic and charlatanism, was very real and very serious. (*SSM*, p. 185)

To his alarm, Merton read the conclusions of Huxley, that, if we wanted to live differently from wild beasts, we must free the spirit by means of prayer and asceticism. The word asceticism had up to now only meant a twisting of nature, but Huxley showed him that it is only through asceticism that the spirit can become itself and find God. Merton shrank from this, but still began hesitatingly to feel out this way.

He bought the first volume of the works of John of the Cross, but actually had no idea where to begin. He wrote:

... These words I underlined, although they amazed and dazzled me with their import, were all too simple for me to understand. They were too naked, too stripped of all duplicity and compromise for my complexity, perverted by many appetites. (*SSM*, pp. 238-39)

Nevertheless, he went on and as soon as he imposed upon himself a strongly ascetical life-style at St. Bonaventure's College, he began to understand even more that "dark night" of the Spanish mystic. At that time, for Merton, saints were still figures who live in bare and impoverished circumstances. In St. Therese of Lisieux he discovered that in the normal civil society the requirements for sainthood and contemplation were also present. He wrote about her:

The one thing that seemed to me more or less impossible was for grace to penetrate the thick, resilient hide of bourgeois smugness and really take hold of the immortal soul beneath that surface, in order to make something out of it. At best, I thought, such people might turn out to be harmless prigs: but great sanctity? Never! . . . However, no sooner had I got a faint glimpse of the real character and the real spirituality of St. Therese, than I was immediately and strongly attracted to her—an attraction that was the work of grace, since, as I say, it took me, in one jump, clean through a thousand psychological obstacles and repugnances. (*SSM*, p. 354)

If it was especially John of the Cross and Therese of Lisieux who brought him in closer contact with Christian mysticism, then it was Ignatius of Loyola who brought him to prayer. The *Spiritual Exercises* had been standing in his bookcase for a long time, but he was a little bit afraid of them, because of ". . . having somewhere acquired a false impression that if you did not look out they would plunge you head first into mysticism before you were aware of it." (*SSM*, p. 268) Still he wanted to try it, and set up his own discipline. He wrote in his autobiography:

As far as I remember, I devoted a whole month to the *Exercises,* taking one hour each day. I took a quiet hour, in the afternoon, in my room on Perry Street: and since I now lived in the back of the house, there were no street noises to worry me. It was really quite silent. With the windows closed, since it was winter, I could not even hear any of the neighborhood's five thousand radios.

The book said the room should be darkened, and I pulled down the blinds so that there was just enough light left for me to see the pages, and to look at the Crucifix on the wall over my bed. And the book also invited me to consider what kind of a position I should take for my meditation. It left me plenty of freedom of choice, so long as I remained more or less the way I was, once I had settled down, and did not go promenading around the room scratching my head and talking to myself.

So I thought and prayed awhile over this momentous problem, and finally decided to make my meditations sitting cross-legged on the floor. I think the Jesuits would have had a nasty shock if they had walked in and seen me doing their *Spiritual Exercises* sitting there like Mahatma Gandhi. But it worked very well. Most of the time

I kept my eyes on the Crucifix or on the floor, when I did not have to look at the book.

And so, having prayed, sitting on the floor, I began to consider the reason why God had brought me into the world. . . . (*SSM*, p. 268-69)

This increasing ease with prayer had a deep effect on the life style of Thomas Merton. Most noticeable was his almost obvious longing for a more disciplined life style, and his growing openness for the beauties of nature. In the beginning his new "rule" was the most visible result. This seemed to come forth almost spontaneously out of his prayer life. He wrote:

I found that, almost without realizing it, I had little by little reorganized the pattern of my life on a stricter plan, getting up earlier in the morning, saying the Little Hours about dawn, or before it when the days got shorter, as a preparation for Mass and Communion. Now, too, I took three quarters of an hour in the morning for mental prayer. I was doing a lot of spiritual reading. . . . (*SSM*, p. 352)

It seemed as if the spiritual freedom which Merton increasingly acquired also made him more open-minded and free in respect to his environment. He was less tense, less agitated, less needy, less restless, and the nature in which he lived—which up to then he had more or less passed by—opened up for him into a beauty which he had never before seen.

It is impressive to see how prayer opens many eyes to nature. Prayer makes men contemplative and attentive. In place of manipulating, the man who prays stands receptive before the world. He no longer grabs but caresses, he no longer bites, but kisses, he no longer examines but admires. To this man, as for Merton, nature can show itself completely renewed. Instead of an obstacle, it becomes a way; instead of an invulnerable shield, it becomes a veil which gives a preview of unknown horizons.

At first Thomas Merton was still too busy with his own inner life to be able to stand completely open to nature. Moreover, how could he experience nature in the city? But whenever he was with his friends in a summer cottage, nature began to speak a language that he never found in books, and his eyes wandered from the words to the trees. He wrote:

> It was a cool summer evening. As I was sitting in the driveway. . . . With the book in my lap I looked down at the lights of the cars crawling up the road from the valley. I looked at the dark outline of the wooded hills and at the stars that were coming out in the eastern sky. The words of the Vulgate text rang and echoed in my heart: *"Qui facit Arcturum et Oriona. . . ;"* "Who makest Arcturus and Orion and Hyades and the inner parts of the South. . . ." (*SSM*, p. 293)

Still these experiences of nature remained exceptional. Books still held his preference. Only later, at the abbey, after living for many years in the Kentucky hills did an intimacy with nature nourish his prayer constantly.

PEOPLE

Next to books, it was especially people who led him to Gethsemani. Despite the fact that *The Secular Journal* and *The Seven Storey Mountain* are full of names of people whom Thomas Merton knew in his youth, there are only a few who stand out as really influential figures. Four names are worthy of our attention: Mark Van Doren, Daniel Walsh, Bramachari and Bob Lax.

Mark Van Doren and Daniel Walsh were both teachers at Columbia. Through their personality and manner of teaching, they created some order in the abundance of ideas and feelings of the young Merton. Remarkably he got to know the two teachers only by chance and he enrolled in their courses, though they were unnecessary for his course of study.

If there was anyone through whom Merton was inspired, it was certainly Mark Van Doren. It is fascinating to read how Merton described this man who in many respects was his teacher. He wrote about Van Doren's lectures in English literature:

It was the best course I ever had at college. And it did me the most good, in many different ways. It was the only place where I ever heard anything really sensible said about any of the things that were really fundamental

—life, death, time, love, sorrow, fear, wisdom, suffering, eternity. . . .

. . . Mark's balanced and sensitive and clear way of seeing things, at once simple and yet capable of subtlety, being fundamentally scholastic, though not necessarily and explicitly Christian, presented these things in ways that made them live within us, and with a life that was healthy and permanent and productive. This class was one of the few things that could persuade me to get on the train and go to Columbia at all. . . . (*SSM*, p. 180)

In Merton's description of Van Doren's teaching method, his picture of the ideal teacher comes out. He said:

. . . Do not think that Mark was simply priming his students with thoughts of his own, and then making the thought stick to their minds by getting them to give it back to him as their own. Far from it. What he did have was the gift of communicating to them something of his own vital interest in things, something of his manner of approach: but the results were sometimes quite unexpected—and by that I mean good in a way that he had not anticipated, casting lights that he had not himself forseen.

Now a man who can go for year after year . . . without having any time to waste in flattering and cajoling his students with any kind of a fancy act, or with jokes, or with storms of temperament, or periodic tirades—whole classes spent in threats and imprecations, to disguise the fact that the professor himself has come in unprepared— one who can do without all these nonessentials both honors his vocation and makes it fruitful. . . . (*SSM*, pp. 139-40)

Daniel Walsh is the second figure at Columbia who meant a lot to Merton. Unlike Mark Van Doren, he was a guest lecturer on Thomas Aquinas at Columbia. He too was described by Merton as an exceptional teacher:

Walsh . . . had nothing of the supercilious self-assurance of the ordinary professor: he did not need this frail and artificial armor for his own insufficiency. He did not need to hide behind tricks and vanities any more than Mark Van Doren did; he never even needed to be brilliant. In his smiling simplicity he used to efface himself entirely in the solid and powerful mind of St. Thomas. . . . (*SSM*, p. 219)

Even before Merton began to attend the lectures of Walsh, he has visited him and presented him with his idea of becoming a priest. Together they talked about all the different orders and eventually settled on the Franciscans as the best type for Merton. But then Walsh told him enthusiastically about Gethsemani and urged him to go there on retreat.

Years later, long after Merton became a Trappist, Walsh came to Gethsemani to teach philosophy, and in 1967 he himself was ordained a priest in the diocese of Louisville.

Both Mark Van Doren and Daniel Walsh were people who radiated a great inner calm. They were not influenced very much by university customs, they were very simple and clear in their lectures, direct and personal in their dealings with students, and were prepared through their vision and personality to create a unity in the thoughts and feelings of the young Merton. Both intellectually and emotionally he found a home with them and he came in contact with a deeper current that was hidden under the surface of a restless student life.

A completely different figure who left a deep influence on Thomas Merton was the Indian monk referred to as Dr. Bramachari (which is the Hindu term for monk). Merton wrote about him with much humor, great respect and deep reverence. When he met Bramachari for the first time at Grand Central Station in New York, he wrote:

> There stood a shy little man, very happy, with a huge smile, all teeth, in the midst of his brown face. And on the top of his head was a yellow turban with Hindu prayers written all over it in red. And, on his feet, sure enough: sneakers. (*SSM*, p. 195)

Merton and Bramachari became friends. Merton admired the sympathetic way in which Bramachari criticized the Western world and relativized everything that men in the university world found so important:

> He was never sarcastic, never ironical or unkind in his criticisms: in fact he did not make many judgments at all, especially adverse ones. He would simply make statements of fact, and then burst out laughing—his laughter was quiet and ingenuous, and it expressed his complete

amazement at the very possibility that people should live the way he saw them living all around him. (*SSM*, p. 196)

Bramachari did not at all try to give Merton an insight into his own belief, let alone to force any convictions on him. On the contrary, he was the one who said to Merton: "There are many beautiful mystical books written by the Christians. You should read St. Augustine's *Confessions,* and *The Imitation of Christ. . . ."* (*SSM,* p. 198)

This was at the very time that Merton was wrestling through the French translation of hundreds of strange Eastern texts. He found them very mysterious and complicated and in the long run they didn't interest him. Thus he was all the more impressed when this Hindu monk pointed him to the Christian mystical tradition. Later he wrote:

> Now that I look back on those days, it seems to me very probable that one of the reasons why God had brought him all the way from India, was that he might say just that. (*SSM*, p. 198)

It seems providential indeed that this Hindu monk relativized Merton's youthful curiosity over the East and made him sensitive to the richness of Western mysticism. Only after he had made this his own, would he be prepared for a real dialogue. But it would still be many years before Merton would meet Daisetz Suzuki, a man whom he judged to be of the same stature as Gandhi and Einstein and who stimulated and enriched his interest in the East. After the contact with Bramachari, the East disappeared from Merton's range of vision, and only after many years of absorption in his own tradition would it reappear on his horizon.

Of all the people who played a role in Merton's journey to Gethsemani, Bob Lax is certainly the most fascinating and perhaps also the central figure. The name of Bob Lax appears most often in *The Seven Storey Mountain* and this remarkable figure emerges time and again at critical moments. He was not the teacher, like Van Doren and Walsh, nor was he as interesting an outsider as Bramachari. He belonged to the small circle of friends with whom Merton spent his student years in New York. Gerdy, Freedgood, Rice, Lax and Merton formed an artistic student club, of which Lax fascinated Merton the most. He was an intimate friend, indeed, but described with so much admiration and sympathy that it is clear how Merton constantly fell under the spell of this mysterious personality.

Remarkable, too, is the fact that Van Doren, Walsh and Bramachari also had come to Merton's attention through Lax, and that Merton continually reveals how much weight Lax's judgments carried for him.

Merton saw Lax for the first time sitting in the midst of a group of editors of the student magazine *Jester*. He wrote:

> Taller than them all, and more serious, with a long face, like a horse, and a great mane of black hair on top of it, Bob Lax meditated on some incomprehensible woe, and waited for someone to come in and begin to talk to them. . . . (SSM, p. 179)

Merton remained fascinated by Lax and tried repeatedly to understand and to describe his complicated personality:

> To name Robert Lax in another way, he was a kind of combination of Hamlet and Elias. A potential prophet, but without rage. A king, but a Jew too. A mind full of tremendous and subtle intuitions, and every day he found less and less to say about them, and resigned himself to being inarticulate. In his hesitations, though without embarrassment or nervousness at all, he would often curl his long legs all around a chair, in seven different ways, while he was trying to find a word with which to begin. He talked best sitting on the floor.
>
> And the secret of his constant solidity I think has always been a kind of natural, instinctive spirituality, a kind of inborn direction to the living God. Lax has always been afraid he was in a blind alley, and half aware that, after all, it might not be a blind alley, but God, infinity.
>
> He had a mind naturally disposed, from the very cradle, to a kind of affinity for Job and St. John of the Cross. And I now know that he was born so much of a contemplative that he will probably never be able to find out how much.
>
> To sum it up, even the people who have always thought he was "too impractical" have always tended to venerate him—in the way people who value material security unconsciously venerate people who do not fear insecurity. (*SSM,* p. 181)

Lax was a Jew, and in many respects he was a prophet for Merton. There is tremendous simplicity and power in their relationship. This becomes visible in a conversation they had walking on Sixth Avenue one spring

evening. Merton recorded the conversation word for
word:

> . . . Lax suddenly turned around and asked me the ques-
> tion:
> L: "What do you want to be, anyway?"
> M: "I don't know; I guess what I want is to be a good
> Catholic."
> L: "What do you mean, you want to be a good Catholic?
> . . . What you should say . . . is that you want to be
> a saint."
> M: "How do you expect me to become a saint?"
> L: "By wanting to."
> M: "I can't be a saint, I can't be a saint. . . ."
> L: "All that is necessary to be a saint is to want to be
> one. Don't you believe that God will make you what
> He created you to be, if you will consent to let Him
> do it? All you have to do is desire it."
> The next day I told Mark Van Doren:
> "Lax is going around saying that all a man needs to be
> a saint is to want to be one."
> "Of course," said Mark.
> All these people were much better Christians than I. They
> understood God better than I. What was I doing? Why
> was I so slow, so mixed up, still, so uncertain in my direc-
> tions and so insecure? (*SSM*, pp. 237–38)

Later, when Merton stood in the monk's choir in the
Trappist Abbey, he discovered Lax among the guests.
When they got together Lax told him that he had become a Catholic. When Lax was teaching at the University of North Carolina, his friend Rice had written
him: "Come to New York and we will find a priest and
ask him to baptize you." Merton wrote:

All of a sudden, after all those years of debating back and forth, Lax just got on a train and went to New York. Nobody had ever put the matter up to him like that before.

They found a Jesuit in that big church up on Park Avenue and he baptized him, and that was that. . . .

Of all the people whom Merton knew in his youth, Lax was undoubtedly the man closest to him. But if that is true, then we can also see how much respect Merton had for him. Lax was his best friend, but he never used him to avoid his deepest feelings of solitude. He describes him more as one of the signs on the way to God.

Perhaps it is indeed a very important aspect of Merton's contemplative spirit that he remained detached from his environment, even from his good friends. He loved them, but didn't use them, he was intensely thankful for everything he received from them, but he didn't attach himself to them. More and more he learned to see his friends as signposts toward God. The power of friendship is great if it doesn't find all of its meaning in itself. If people expect too much from each other, they can do each other harm; and disappointment and bitterness can overpower love and even replace it. Already as a student in New York Merton didn't try to avoid solitude. While his friends were often busy with all sorts of activities, he sought out a quiet place for prayer. In this silence he got to know God and also learned to value and admire his friends. Lax, in fact, meant so much to Merton because he found in him just what he had discovered in silence. Merton could only call Lax a born mystic because he himself had experienced who God is, the one who spoke to him in silence.

It is this silence which became fuller and deeper for Merton: first as member of a monastic community, then as hermit. It is important to see that it is this experience of God in silence that put Merton more and more in a position to recognize both God and the devil in people and events around him. The silence prepared him to understand everything he saw as a possible sign on the way to a new world.

EVENTS

We have described books and people as signs on the way to silence. The more we reflect on this, the clearer it becomes that we cannot really understand God's work with man. In the final analysis people do not explain much to us. They are but signs which lead us to suspect something unspeakably great. This is also true for the events about which we now want to speak. Millions have experienced these same events, but for Merton they became signs on the way. Here we refer specifically to the second world war. A year after it broke out—in 1939—Merton entered the Trappists. The premonitions of the war and the ominous beginning preoccupied him intensely. His diaries make this very clear and in his novel *My Argument with the Gestapo,* the problem of war and peace is central. How personal a thing it was for Merton appears in the characterization which he himself gave to his novel: ". . . a . . . sardonic meditation on the world in which I then found myself: an attempt to define its predicament and my own place in it" (*MA,* p. 6)

The atmosphere of war had a deep influence on Merton and probably hastened his way to the abbey. The war forced him to pose the fundamental question which otherwise may have long remained suppressed: How can I be a man of peace? He began to understand more clearly the gripping urge of destruction all around him as an invitation to voluntarily become nothing. The craving to conquer more land and more goods became for him an invitation to voluntarily take his distance from all possessions and to go naked through life. The blind violence that tore the world from its joints, became for him an appeal to follow the path of nonviolence and to accept all the consequences.

On June 16, 1940 he wrote in his diary:

> Therefore, if I don't pretend, like other people, to understand the war, I do know this much: that the knowledge of what is going on only makes it seem desperately important to be voluntarily poor, to get rid of all possessions this instant. I am scared, sometimes, to own anything, even a name, let alone coin, or shares in the oil, the munitions, the airplane factories. I am scared to take a proprietary interest in anything, for fear that my love of what I own may be killing somebody somewhere. (*SJ*, p. 98)

A year later, after Merton had his first extended contact with Trappist life, this insight became deeper. He began to see more clearly that self-imposed poverty not only prevents violence, but also makes one completely free to work in the middle of danger. Detachment in poverty is more than a means to prevent one's

fellow-man from suffering conscious or unconscious violence. It offers the unheard of chance to stand without
fear in a violent world. This is the new insight that
already appeared in the novel that he wrote in the summer of 1941. To the question of whether he is afraid
in this dangerous world, the main character, Merton
himself, answers:

> I know I am in danger, but how can I be afraid of dan-
> ger? If I remember I am nothing, I will know the danger
> can take nothing from me. . . . Yes, I am afraid, because
> I forget that I am nothing. If I remembered that I have
> nothing called my own that will not be lost anyway, that
> only what is not mine but God's will ever live, then I
> would not fear so many false fears. (*MA*, p. 138)

Here a new life ideal becomes visible. Detachment
does not mean shirking one's responsibilities. Rather it
is a supremely active deed which makes it possible to
move unprejudiced and unafraid into the center of the
evil, where one destroys what one really possesses and
uses violence in the false presupposition that life means
power. The poor man can enter into this center with
nonviolence because he has nothing to defend and he
can destroy evil at its root.

The self-emptied man is revolutionary in the real
sense because he claims nothing—not even his life—as
his possession and therefore he can take away the false
basis of war and violence by refusing every compromise with possessions.

We find the start of these thoughts in the young
Merton who searches for his answer to the second world

war. It is therefore not surprising that we see Merton later as one of the most important writers on non-violence, as one of the best interpreters of Gandhi, and as the one who constantly questions what *kenosis*, self-emptying, means for the modern man or woman.

Books, people and events: we have described these as signs on the way to silence. They do not give an explanation of his call, but are only symptoms of it. Gilson, Huxley, John of the Cross, Therese of Lisieux, Ignatius of Loyola—he discovered them in literature and experimented with their ideas. Mark Van Doren, Daniel Walsh, Bramachari and Bob Lax—he met them in New York and experienced God's love in their friendship. The events of the second world war—they formed the context in which he read the books and met the people, supported his vague premonitions and quickened his personal decision.

It is perhaps always a bit disappointing when we look for an answer to the question of God in our lives. We are left only with titles of books, names of people and a few old facts. It seems all a bit lean and superficial. God doesn't let Himself get caught in titles, names and facts. But He lets Himself be suspected. And therefore it is only the one who prays to God, quite possibly the one who searches for silence himself, who can recognize Him in the many little ideas, meetings and happenings on the way to silence.

CHAPTER 3

Conquering Solitude

Thomas Merton wrote about himself in the years before he became a Trappist as if he were writing about a journalist, not only because he was writing for different magazines but also because for him the concept "journalist" had a particular meaning. This appears clearest in his novel *My Argument with the Gestapo*, in which he himself is the main character. He comes back to a bombed-out London where he had lived as a student. He appears there as a journalist but not in the sense that the people around him think of a journalist. To be sure, he observes and reports. He is in the thick of the happenings. He writes down what he hears, sees, smells and tastes; but the question "What is important?" has a different meaning for him than for his colleagues who must provide the home front with news. He is a journalist, a reporter, but a journalist who stops at everyday things and asks what their sense and meaning are. The terrible suffering, death and destruction that he sees are new for him in the sense that they formulate in a completely new way the question of the meaning of life and death. The opinions of police and military are no explanation for him; peace conferences and armistices are no real signs of hope.

Merton's questions are: "What is peace? What is justice? What is love? Are we ready for this?" And especially, "What is *my* place in the middle of this chaotic and noisy world?" This last question led him to the silence of Gethsemani. In this silence where he lived for twenty-seven years, he in fact remained a journalist, a reporter who observes the world in which he lived, but under the critical eye of the gospel.

In the years which Merton spent in the Trappist monastery, he wrote an enormous amount, at least 35 books and an impressive number of articles, not to mention the many works (journals, letters, etc.) that are not yet published, many of which are appearing posthumously. When we look at all this work, it appears that the great power of Merton as a writer still remains in his ability to comment on the concrete happenings of the day, and to do this out of a contemplative silence. He never wrote great systematic works, and his most objective work is often his weakest. Therefore in the long run his diaries and his short commentaries may prove to belong to his most important contributions.

In Gethsemani Merton wrote many diaries, two of which have been published: *Conjectures of a Guilty Bystander,* which he kept during the years 1956-1965,

and *The Sign of Jonas* which covers the years 1942-
1952. We must look to them for an understanding of
how he grew in his newly acquired solitude.

In many respects *The Sign of Jonas* is a monologue,
in which Merton—finally a Trappist—now really tries
to conquer the solitude to which he was led by many
signs. It is an impressive book because it describes
the painful wrestling of man with God. And, in a very
convincing manner, it demonstrates that the walls of an
abbey are certainly no guarantee for solitude and inner
silence. But this all means that Merton himself in many
instances stands in the center of *The Sign of Jonas*. It is
an honest, but also anxious, adventure in self-revelation
and self-discovery. Up to now the question was: "Where
is my place in the world?" The answer was: "In solitude." Now the question is: "What is my place in
solitude?" This has been the subject of a long struggle
written down in a diary which on first reading may seem
boring, but by further study illustrates an exceptionally
fascinating development.

His second diary, *Conjectures of a Guilty Bystander*
is completely different in its style and content. Merton
calls it "a personal version of the world in the 1960s."
He writes:

> . . . These notes . . . are an implicit dialogue with other
> minds, a dialogue in which questions are raised. But do
> not expect to find "my answers." I do not have clear an-
> swers to current questions. I do have questions, and, as a
> matter of fact, I think a man is known better by his ques-
> tions than by his answers. (*CGB*, p. v)

The subject of this diary is not Merton himself but his reactions to the books he read, to the people he spoke with, and the events which he heard about. The titles of the parts of the two diaries show a clear difference. In *The Sign of Jonas,* the parts are called: "Solemn Profession," "Death of an Abbot," "Major Orders," and, "To the Altar of God." In *Conjectures of a Guilty Bystander* we find other titles such as: "Barth's Dream," "Truth and Violence," "The Madman Runs to the East," and so on.

This development is very important. Just as we can only enter into a real intimate relation with one another when we first get to know our own identities, often, after much pain and suffering, so Merton was really in the position to occupy himself critically with his world only after he had found his own solitude. *The Sign of Jonas* can in many ways be described as the adolescence of a contemplative, in which the spiritual identity crisis must be brought to a solution. As often as a man ventures to a deeper, more fundamental level of life in trying to give form to his life, he exposes himself to a crisis which is more painful and heart-rending. In this sense a man has just as many adolescences as he takes risks to *fathom* his life.

Shortly before his death, Thomas Merton was asked by the Holy See to collaborate on a message to the world on the meaning of the contemplative life. Merton had no time for a systematic description, but answered immediately with a personal letter which was widely publicized. In this he said:

The contemplative has nothing to tell you except to re-
assure you and say that if you dare to penetrate your own
silence and dare to advance without fear into the solitude of your own heart, and risk the sharing of that solitude with the lonely other who seeks God through you
and with you, then you will truly recover the light and
the capacity to understand what is beyond words and
beyond explanations because it is too close to be explained: it is the intimate union in the depths of your
own heart, of God's spirit and your own secret inmost
self, so that you and He are in all truth One Spirit. (Letter
21st August 1967)

These words which seem so simple and obvious were
written against a background of a life's journey in which
they had become the flesh and blood of the one who
wrote them. Thus, the conquering of silence and solitude by Merton is also of real importance in understanding his role in a discussion of violence and nonviolence and in appreciating his contribution to the
dialogue with the Eastern mystics.

If we now want to look further into Thomas Merton's
struggles for solitude, then we must begin with the
sober statement that Thomas Merton, who entered the
Trappists to find rest and silence, in fact ended up in
a particularly busy, restless and noisy situation. The
world war had confronted not only Merton but also
many other young Americans, who had come to know
the world from its cruelest side, with the question of
the meaning of existence. The result was that in the
years 1940-1950 the Abbey of Gethsemani grew from

70 to 270 members. Merton comments, a little sourly, "Thus two hundred and seventy lovers of silence and solitude are all packed into a building that was built for seventy." (*SOJ*, p. 14)

That meant new training courses, new buildings, the preparation for new foundations and so forth; much talk and debate, many discussions and lectures, many tractors and bulldozers, and the constant going in and coming out of busy monks. Merton called Gethsemani, in those days, a "furnace of ambivalence."

In this context, then, we must also look at the question which completely dominated the first part of *The Sign of Jonas:* "Am I here in my place? Should I not enter the Carthusians, or just become a common hermit?" This is a search for silence, yet also the question of one whose inner turmoil made him desire more hours of calm than the abbey could offer him at that time. The youthful enthusiasm and generosity with which he wanted to give himself to God without reservation were so frustrated that he thought he could never reach his vocation at Gethsemani. He wanted more solitude and more silence. But his own restlessness and his relatively busy life in the abbey made him wonder whether he was called to a purely contemplative life. His abbot and spiritual director encouraged him more and more to write. Meanwhile he had to do much work in the fields and he received other jobs from all sides. In this situation he began to question whether his longing for solitude wasn't perhaps a self-seeking, egoistic desire. He wrote: "It is not important to live for contemplation, but for God." He began to question his motives and at the same time found his only foothold in obedience to his superiors who said that he was in his place in the abbey.

In this crisis a new light broke through. It was the discovery of the contemplative value of what seems common routine, and of the doubtful value of all feelings of delight and spiritual satisfaction. Solitude can be sought and found in the routine of the simple world, in which man can be alone in his heart. "But this desert is not necessarily a geographical one. It is a solitude of heart in which created joys are consumed and reborn in God." (*SOJ*, p. 59)

During this time Merton also made another discovery: that contemplation doesn't mean learning about contemplation: that silence isn't thinking, learning and talking about silence—and that solitude doesn't mean a heartful of beautiful thoughts about being alone with God. With great honesty he uncovered his own intellectualism and his rational approach to his problems. He said to himself:

> Here is what you need to do more and more—shut up about all that—architecture, Spirit of the Order, contemplation, liturgy, chant—be simple and poor or you will never have any peace. . . . (*SOJ*, p. 122)

It is at this time that his temptation to become a Carthusian crept up in the background. But then, too, a new level of solitude was beginning to develop in him which he could put into words only with difficulty. It was a solitude which invited him to be no longer busy with himself, no longer concerned over what he did or had to do, no longer to want to hold in his own hands the way to solitude. At that moment, too, his vision of his vocation as an author changed. Instead of a handicap, his writing became an entrance to real silence and solitude. Writing in fact became for him the only way to sanctity. "If I am to be a saint," he writes, "I must also put down on paper what I have become . . . to put myself down on paper . . . with the most complete simplicity and integrity, masking nothing. . . ." (*SOJ,* p. 288-9)

In his work as a writer, Merton discovered also a new experience of poverty. By his writing he had made himself and his most inner feelings and thoughts a public possession. In this way he had disowned himself and allowed others to enter in his monastic silence. In this way his fame had made him spiritually poor. But this same poverty made the world around him appear to him in a new way. It seems as if everything belonged to him just when there was nothing left to him which he could call his "private property." The air, the trees, the whole world, were now singing the honor of God and he felt fire and music in the earth under his feet. The beauty of creation made him poor and wealthy at the same time and gave him peace and happiness. This beauty kept him from wanting to experience nature as a possession, but helped him to deeply experience his silence and solitude.

But this solitude and rest were cruelly disturbed during a period of terrible anxiety and uncertainty. In December, 1949, Merton wrote, desperate as a sick and depressed person who has lost his orientation and feels completely alienated from himself: "It is fear that is driving me into solitude." (*SOJ,* p. 248) It seemed as if everything were broken to pieces and as if nothing were left of the beautiful contemplative ideals. "I am exhausted by fear," (*SOJ,* p. 248) he wrote. After eight years of life in the monastery, he felt miserable, sinful, guilty and without any prospects. The solitude was now felt as harsh, difficult and painful and gave him the experience of being empty and even totally "nothing."

But then, at the depth of his misery, he again found God and his fellow human beings. When everything was dark, he found himself in God's own solitude. In the winter of 1950 he wrote:

> True solitude is a participation in the solitariness of God— Who is in all things. His solitude is not a local absence but a metaphysical transcendence. . . . (*SOJ,* p. 262)

This heavy darkness appeared to be a purification which prepared him for a new task. In May, 1951 Merton became the spiritual director for the students. That is the Sign of Jonas. God called Jonas to go to the people, but Jonas fled to solitude until God let him be brought back through the whale to where his real calling lay. Merton said then, too, "like Jonas himself, I find myself traveling toward my destiny in the belly of a paradox." (*SOJ,* p. 21) But when he stood before his students he discovered that something great had happened to him. The silence and solitude had buried themselves so deeply in his heart that he was in the position to take on a very deep and intimate relation with other persons. Perhaps most moving in *The Sign of Jonas* is the development of compassion in solitude. In silence Merton discovered humanity once again. The new name for the desert in which he saw many of his self-constructed ambitions destroyed was: compassion. He learned to feel and respect silence in the life of another. He learned there to love his brothers, not for what they say but for what they are. He saw now, with amazement, the quietude and solitude that lived in them. Now he wanted only to be a man among people, a member of humanity—no more, no less ridiculous than himself.

The conquering of silence also gave him a new task: to share this silence with others. But that required no special effort because:

> . . . Once God has called you to solitude, everything you touch leads you further into solitude. (*SOJ*, p. 323)

And now Merton dared to write:

> There is no wilderness so terrible, so beautiful, so arid and so fruitful as the wilderness of compassion. It is the only desert that shall truly flourish like the lily. . . . (*SOJ*, p. 323)

In this deepest solitude which became compassion, one is no longer examined. Curiosity turns into admiration, direction turns into guidance, and silence becomes a place where no one has to ask questions, but all can really be together in God.

And so ends the first diary written in the abbey. Merton was the reporter of his own inner life. He put his daily feelings and thoughts under the critical eye of the gospel, and in the depth of solitude he found God and his fellow human beings. This cleansing was necessary before he could detach himself from his preoccupations to touch the world, which was being wrenched apart by racial discrimination, violence and poverty, with the hand of compassion.

CHAPTER 4

Unmasking the Illusion

Above one of the doors of the abbey, the words: "God alone" are carved in the stone. That was what Merton wanted; a way from the wild business of the hustling world, which sought happiness where it couldn't be found. Away from the many discussions and defenses and arguments over things which didn't go any further than self-interest. Away from the novels, reports and stories with which he had wanted to make himself popular. Away from the movies and bars which numbed the senses and the source of life. Away into the silence of the abbey, the rest of nature, the regularity of the prayer life, there to be with "God alone."

But this romantic life, in which a real seeking for God lay hidden, couldn't remain romantic for very long. It is fascinating to read how Thomas Merton is followed his whole life long with the rumor that he had left the monastery, that he had not persevered, that he was no longer a monk or a priest, that he was married, or had disappeared to another country. When *The Seven Storey Mountain* was published, it was already said that he would soon leave, and Merton was constantly tormented by the sick hope of some of his readers that he would not persevere. To many it sounded too beautiful, too pious, too sensational. Even many of the faithful suggested that for a romantic such as Merton it was impossible to persevere in any monastery, especially in a Trappist community.

Perhaps there was still a kernel of truth in all these reports, insofar as Merton indeed had to be purified in solitude to become a real monk. The "God alone" had to first be shaken from all traces of false romanticism and of flight from the evil world, in order to really be able to bear fruit. In *The Sign of Jonas* we find a part of this purification described. Soon he learned to see that becoming a Carthusian would not help him in his search for real solitude and silence, that solitude is primarily a quality of the heart, and that solitude would become false when its social dimension is not recognized.

Perhaps Merton's most important discovery was the discovery of his fellowman at the depths of his own solitude. He experienced a new solidarity in the depths of his silence and he seemed to find there, where he was most alone, the basis of community. In silence his mockery became generosity, his self-conceit became solidarity, his sarcasm became compassion. On March 3,

1951, when he had been in Gethsemani for ten years, he wrote about his life in solitude:

> And now I owe everyone else in the world a share in that life. My first duty is to start, for the first time, to live as a member of a human race which is no more (and no less) ridiculous than I am myself. And my first human act is the recognition of how much I owe everybody else. (*SOJ*, p. 312)

Through purification and solitude, "God alone" became "together with all men." In silence Merton discovered that being a monk is preeminently a social calling. This conviction became more mature after 1951 when Merton became spiritual director for the students. In the 1960s when racial strife burst loose in all its vehemence, when the conscience of America suffered under Vietnam, when poverty became more apparent, Merton was one of the most influential voices to which people listened in order to find some light in the darkness, and some clarity in the midst of the confusion of spirit.

On the 10th of December 1968, a few hours before his death, Merton gave a lecture in Bangkok on Marxism and Monasticism. In this he recounted:

> I was at a meeting to which many revolutionary university leaders from France, Italy, Germany, the Low Countries, had been invited. This meeting took place in Santa Barbara, California. . . . In a lull between conferences I was speaking informally with some of those students, and I introduced myself as a monk, and one of the French

revolutionary students immediately said: "We are monks also. . . ." The monk is essentially someone who takes up a critical attitude towards the contemporary world and its structures. . . . But the criticism is undoubtedly quite different . . . the student seemed to be alluding to the fact that if one is to call himself in one way or another a monk he must have in some way or other reached some kind of critical conclusion about the validity of certain claims made by secular society and its structures with regard to the end of man's existence. ("Marxist Theory and Monastic Theories", p. 2)

This story displays Merton's deep conviction that contemplation is basically a social matter, and that silence, solitude, prayer, are not private properties, but belong to the people with and for whom he lives. His conviction that solitude didn't belong to him as a possession came forth out of his heart-rending discovery that Auschwitz, Hiroshima, Vietnam and Watts were present in the intimate core of his own being. There where he thought he could be alone with himself, he found that he wasn't one man, but that in him lived mankind, in all its misery but also in its longing for love. And out of this self-examination the call came forth to put into words his own deepest experience and to offer it to others for reflection, because this experience wasn't a private matter; rather, it was often the unspoken and unreflected experience of all humanity.

How Merton personally experienced this appears in the fact that his own historicity reveals itself to him as a heavy obligation.

That I should have been born in 1915, that I should be the contemporary of Auschwitz, Hiroshima, Vietnam and the Watts riots are things about which I was not first consulted. Yet they are also events in which, whether I like it or not, I am deeply and personally involved. (*CWA*, p. 145)

This experience brought Merton to the conviction that a choice was being demanded of him. If his own history contained a calling, he could accept or throw it off. And the tragedy of it is that the religious, the monk, the Christian threatens to repudiate his calling under the mantle of scorning the world. He wrote:

To choose the world is . . . first of all an acceptance of a task and a vocation in the world, in history and in time. And it has now become transparently obvious that mere automatic "rejection of the world" and "contempt for the world" is in fact not a choice but the evasion of choice. The man who pretends that he can turn his back on Auschwitz or Vietnam and act as if they were not there is simply bluffing. I think that this is getting to be generally admitted, even by monks. (*CWA*, p. 149)

But for Merton these thoughts meant in no way that he now would be better off to leave Gethsemani in order to actively engage in the civil rights or peace movements, to take part in demonstrations, to support draft resisters and to sound his protesting voice everywhere. So thought his readers who felt that a man who thought and wrote as Merton did belonged in the front line of the action and not in the garden of a monastery. But on this very point he was not understood. In one of his last letters from India he still found it necessary to write: "I hope there are not too many crazy rumors. Keep telling everyone that I am a monk of Gethsemani and intend to remain one all my days." (Asian Letters 1968)

In this light it is even more important to understand the kind of rebellion to which Merton wanted to dedicate himself. His vocation as monk was neither to fight on the front lines, nor to turn his back on the world with contempt. His task was not the denial of a reality, but the unmasking of an illusion. He wrote:

> The world as pure object is something that is not there. It is not a reality outside us for which we exist. . . . It is a living and self-creating mystery of which I am myself a part, to which I am myself, my own unique door. When I find the world in my own ground, it is impossible for me to be alienated by it. (*CWA*, p. 154-5)

Merton understood that the unmasking of illusion belonged to the essence of the contemplative life. The many years of prayer and solitude had confronted him with his own illusions. But through this he was also prepared to show himself and his fellow human beings that which they would rather keep hidden. This unmasking is not a game that one can choose to play or not to play. It is a sacred duty, and regards the here and now of what occurs in this world. In his *Seeds of Destruction*, where he reveals himself as a sharp critic of society, he wrote:

. . . We are bound to search "history," that is to say the intelligible actions of men, for some indications of their inner significance, and some relevance to our commitment as Christians. (*SD*, p. 18)

In the years 1960 to 1968 "history" meant for Merton: the killing of children in Birmingham and civil-rights workers in Mississippi; the killing of Mrs. Liuzzo and the Unitarian minister in Selma, Alabama; the burning of churches in the South, the riots in Watts, Newark, Chicago, Cleveland; the long march from Selma to Montgomery and the dramatic march to Washington where Martin Luther King spoke of his dream. These were events which followed upon each other in quick succession and threatened the unity of a great land.

In 1963 the president was assassinated; in 1964-65 black leaders were killed by snipers. The figure of King came forward as a sign of hope and thousands walked with him in nonviolent protest. But when he was assassinated in 1967 and buried in Atlanta, nonviolence seemed to be buried with him and black power alone remained as an alternative. The hot summer of 1967 began with fires in Detroit and Chicago and a growing fear of chaos. In June, 1968, Robert Kennedy was assassinated, the one white leader who still gave hope to the blacks. And after this the country fell lame and tired, waiting for a restoration which would give power to continue the battle with a much greater vehemence. Murder, hate, anarchy, chaos, desperation, despair, a people full of anxiety—these were the signs of America.

In every subway in New York policemen walked; a taxi driver refused to ride through certain areas after sundown. Parents did not dare let their children go alone to school. Meanwhile there came more factories, chimneys and cars, covering the cities with a reddish-brown haze and threatening the health of their inhabitants. About all this Merton said: "We are bound to search the intelligible actions of men, for some indications of their inner significance." (*SD*, p. 18)

It would be unfair to say that Merton had an exclusive interest in the racial question. He was passionately interested in his whole world and that meant for him the racial question, as well as international politics, the student protests, conscientious objection to war, and the many peace movements. He was interested in these current problems, not as one who might take part in an action group, but in order to search in his own silence for the inner meaning and message that they held for the Christian.

In a letter written in the summer of 1968 he summarized his convictions when he wrote:

I am against war, against violence, against violent revolution, for peaceful settlement of differences, for nonviolent but nevertheless radical changes. Change is needed, and violence will not really change anything: at most it will only transfer power from one set of bull-headed authorities to another. If I say these things, it is not because I am more interested in politics than in the Gospel. I am not. But today more than ever the Gospel commitment has political implications, because you cannot claim to be "for Christ" and espouse a political cause that implies callous indifference to the needs of millions of human beings and even cooperate in their destruction. (Midsummer Letter 1968)

That was tough language for a monk, but for Merton it was necessary language in order to be a monk and remain one. He could speak this language, because he had been able to test his experiences in solitude with that which he saw and read about his times. The racial questions stood undoubtedly in the center but precisely because he judged this struggle not from a strategical political point of view but from his experience of the gospel. His criticism took on a dimension which went far above the interests of a state or country. For he was concerned here once again with the unmasking of human illusions and not merely with some ideological standpoint. Merton's vision of the racial problem is most sharply expressed in his book *Seeds of Destruction,* especially in his "Letters to a White Liberal." Some deeper reflections of his attitude reside in his introduction to a number of texts of Gandhi, published under the title *Gandhi on Nonviolence.* These two studies deserve particular attention because they give us a good introduction to Merton as a critic of society.

In order to better understand Merton's unmasking of the illusion we must put two figures in the foreground, James Baldwin and Mahatma Gandhi. Both figures had a great influence on Merton and prepared him to put into words what he had experienced in silence. James Baldwin is the black author who in his books *Go Tell it on the Mountain, Another Country,* and *The Fire Next Time,* shows in a shocking manner that the black problem in fact is a problem of the whites. In a letter to Baldwin, Merton said:

> ... I am glad I am not a Negro because I probably would never be able to take it: but ... I recognize in conscience that I have a duty to try to make my fellow whites stop doing things they do and see the problem in a different light. (*SD,* p. 210)

Baldwin showed him that different light and much that Merton said about the racial question was influenced by his ideas. In his "Letters to a White Liberal," Merton addresses himself with frightening sharpness to the progressive citizen who was in favor of integration.

> Now, my liberal friend, here is your situation. You, the well-meaning liberal, are right in the middle of all this confusion. You are, in fact, a political catalyst. On the other hand, with your good will and your ideals, your fine hopes and your generous, but vague, love of mankind in the abstract and of rights enthroned on a juridical Olympus, you offer a certain encouragement to the Negro (and you do right, my only complaint being that you are not yet right enough) so that, abetted by you, he is emboldened to demand concessions. Though he knows you will not support all his demands, he is well aware that you will be forced to support some of them in order to maintain your image of yourself as a liberal. He also knows, however, that your material comforts, your security, and your congenial relations with the establish-

ment are much more important to you than your rather volatile idealism, and that when the game gets rough you will be quick to see your own interests menaced by his demands. And you will sell him down the river for the five hundredth time in order to protect yourself. For this reason, as well as to support your own self-esteem, you are very anxious to have a position of leadership and control in the Negro's fight for rights, in order to be able to apply the brakes when you feel it is necessary. (*SD*, 33-34)

Merton thought about the situation in his own land in all its consequences. The roots of destruction and violence lay in whites themselves and also in the so-called "nigger-lovers" because they are for integration and fight for it as long as they don't feel that their own lives and that of their society require a radical change. As long as whites don't want to look deeply into their own heart and turn into themselves, all their good intentions for the black will remain only flirtations, and all their so-called help only apparent concessions. An oppressed people cannot be controlled very long with artificial means, and it might just be that the white liberals, who want to help everyone but will not change themselves, in fact are preparing the way for revolution. For it is just such whites who at a certain moment will say, "but now we are going too far," and instead of a nonviolent Christian he will become a violent fascist. Merton saw it in somber colors:

At the end of this chain of thought I visualize you, my liberal friend, goose-stepping down Massachusetts Avenue in the uniform of an American Totalitarian Party in a mass rally where nothing but the most uproarious approval is manifest, except, by implication, on the part of silent and strangely scented clouds of smoke drifting over from the new "camps" where the "Negroes are living in retirement." (*SD*, p. 38)

The white Americans who speak with horror about the persecution of the Jews are at the point of setting up their own concentration camps because they refuse to recognize the evil in their land and come to conversion. The sense of the nonviolent protest of the blacks is not to give the blacks a place in a corrupt society which they themselves have condemned to death, but to wake up the conscience of whites and to confront them with their own injustice and sin. Merton said:

> . . . the irony is that the Negro . . . is offering the white man a "message of salvation," but the white man is so blinded by his self-sufficiency and self-conceit that he does not recognize the peril in which he puts himself by ignoring the offer. (*SD*, p. 53)

Where do whites earn the conceit to think that the blacks want to adopt their values and ideas? The black is sent as a prophet who is unrecognized. Merton wrote:

> The Negro . . . is inviting us to understand him as necessary to our own lives. . . . He is warning us that we cannot do without him, and that if we insist on regarding him as an enemy, an object of contempt or a rival, we will perhaps sterilize and ruin our own lives. He is telling us that unless we can enter into a vital and Christian relationship with him, there will be hate, violence and

civil war indeed: and from this violence perhaps none of us will emerge whole. (*SD*, pp. 52-53)

The fires, destruction, death and riots are a *kairos*, an historic opportunity for the whites to finally confess their guilt and to convert themselves. If they do not understand their time as *kairos* and reject the offer of the black, only revolution, violence and destruction can follow, and the period of nonviolence will be followed by a disastrous explosion of violence.

Merton wrote that in 1963 when "Black Power" did not exist. The well-known American theologian Martin E. Marty attacked him vociferously. How did a monk, someone sitting safely behind the walls of a Trappist monastery, dare to take on the robe of a prophet and predict a period of violence. But in the summer of 1967 when the American cities were in flames and Stokely Carmichael had launched his Black Power movement, Marty wrote that the monk Merton understood the situation of his country more deeply and fundamentally than he himself and he offered a public apology for his rash criticism.

Merton didn't even think about saying "You see, I was right." On the contrary, in 1968, he was still hopeful. He spoke then of the last chance the whites were being offered. But when the blacks looted stores in an irrational frenzy and hurt themselves more than they did the whites he wrote:

The Negro has in some sense abandoned the struggle for Civil Rights. He has given up Christian nonviolence as

futile idealism. He has decided that whitey only understands one kind of language: violence. The Negro has
concluded that if whitey wants to terrorize the Vietnamese with napalm and other cozy instruments of war,
he should have a little taste of what fire and terror feel
like at home. So in effect the Negro is declaring guerilla
war on white society. (*FV*, p. 175)

It seemed as if the summer of 1967 had taken away
much of Merton's hope. Violence led to violence and
a police state seemed to be a definite possibility, one
in which the white extremists had the upper hand and
would let their cruelty take a free rein. That then is
the unmasking of the illusion of an integration without
reform. The blacks have let the whites see themselves
by forcing them to draw the final consequences out of
their hardness of heart. In this situation Merton could
only hope against all hope:

> And I do hope we will keep our heads enough to prevent
> a complete polarization . . . which makes all reasonable
> communication between the races impossible . . . if Chris-
> tianity is being discredited in the eyes of Negroes, that
> does not dispense us from our duty to be authentic Chris-
> tians towards the Negro whether he likes us or not. (*FV*,
> p. 179)

This sounds like the voice of one who is a witness to
the bankruptcy of Christianity but refuses to give in to
the temptation to deny the Lord himself. But Merton
did not become bitter. On the contrary he knew that
he was dealing with a question that penetrated so
deeply into the core of human existence, where good

and evil find their sources, that every longing for a direct visible result was a sign of little faith.

Bitterness is the reaction of one who expects something from another without daring to look into his or her own heart, and therefore becomes quickly disappointed. Merton knew only too well that the sin, evil and violence that he found in the world, were the same sin, the same evil, and the same violence that he had discovered in his own heart through solitude, silence, and prayer. The impurity in the world was a mirror of the impurity in his own heart. Perhaps it was just the failure of nonviolence in his country which brought Merton to a growing interiorization and brought him to the conclusion that nonviolence quickly degenerates into tactics and strategy when one still carries traces of violence in one's heart. The only one who has the right to speak about nonviolence, is the one who wants to cleanse himself of all violence through fasting, penance, and prayer. If it was Baldwin who helped Merton to see that the black problem was essentially a problem of the white, it was Gandhi who cautioned him not to become a bitter idealist and taught him again and again to turn to his own interiority.

The teaching of Gandhi made a deep impression on Merton and influenced his thought strongly. Moreover it was Gandhi who set him on the path to the East. Merton wrote:

> . . . the radical difference between him and other leaders, even the most sincere and honest of them, becomes evident by the fact that Gandhi is chiefly concerned with

truth and with service, svadharma, rather than with the possible success of his tactics upon other people, and paradoxically it was his religious conviction that made Gandhi a great politician rather than a mere tactician or operator. (*SD*, p. 161)

It is easy to understand why Merton felt so much at home with Gandhi, when we consider that it was precisely in his solitude that Merton had discovered the possibility of a compassion, which in essence is nonviolent. Nonviolence then, according to Merton, is not a method to achieve something that is already achieved. Baldwin had never said this, but only remarked that the black was nonviolent, not in order to conquer something, but in order to convert the white. Merton saw now that nonviolence indeed was not the searching for results but was the inherent quality of spiritual unity which one himself achieved. The creative spirit of unity which one can find in the silence of one's own heart is not a strictly personal possession, but the life of the spirit of all men and women. Therefore, releasing this spirit—which can also be called truth—is a service to all of humanity. That is not to say that one helps one's fellow human beings by withdrawing in silence. For by seeking truth and justice together with one's fellow human beings one can discover and free this truth in oneself.

One of the deepest of Merton's insights which he formulated in the book *Gandhi on Nonviolence,* is that the spirit of truth is the spirit of nonviolence. The Spirit of truth reveals to us that our present situation is not definitive but rather carries within itself the possibility of conversion to the good. Merton wrote:

> Hence nonviolence implies a kind of bravery far different from violence. In the use of force, one simplifies the situation by assuming that the evil to be overcome is clear-cut, definite, and irreversible. Hence there remains but one thing: to eliminate it. Any dialogue with the sinner, any question of the irreversibility of his act, only means faltering and failure. Failure to eliminate evil is itself a defeat. . . . The greatest of tyrannies are all therefore based on the postulate that *there should never be any sin.* (*G,* pp. 13-14)

Here Merton touched the core of nonviolence. Nonviolence stands or falls according to the vision of evil. If evil is seen only as an irreversible, clearly visible and sharply outlined tumor, then there is only one possibility: cut it out. And then violence is necessary. But when evil is reversible and can be turned into good through forgiveness, then nonviolence is a possibility. Since Merton had experienced in his own life that forgiveness is possible through Christ, nonviolence became then not only a possibility, but even a prerequisite for being Christian.

In a very impressive way, Merton showed how this nonviolence can give form to a new community. He said:

> A violent change would not have been a serious change at all. To punish and destroy the oppressor is merely to initiate a new cycle of violence and oppression. The only

real liberation is that which *liberates both the oppressor and the oppressed* at the same time from the same tyrannical automatism of the violent process which contains in itself the curse of irreversibility. . . . True freedom is then inseparable from the inner strength which can assume the common burden of evil which weighs both on oneself and one's adversary. False freedom is only a manifestation of the weakness that cannot bear even one's evil until it is projected on the other and seen as exclusively his. The highest form of spiritual freedom is, as Gandhi believed, to be sought in the strength of heart which is capable of liberating the oppressed and the oppressor together. But in any event, the oppressed must be able to be free within himself, so that he may begin to gain strength to pity his oppressor. . . . (*G,* pp. 14-15)

Here we have come back to the compassion that must be formed in one's heart, a compassion that comes out of a deep experience of solidarity, in which one recognizes that the evil, sin and violence which one sees in the world and in the other, are deeply rooted in one's own heart. Only when you want to confess this and want to rely on the merciful God who can bring good out of evil are you in a position to receive forgiveness and also to give it to other men and women who threaten you with violence. Precisely because Merton had discovered this nonviolent compassion in his solitude could he in a real sense be a monk, that is to say, one who unmasks through his criticism the illusions of a violent society and who wants to change the world in spirit and truth.

CHAPTER 5

Discovery of the East

In the Preface to the Japanese edition of *The Seven Storey Mountain*, twenty years after the first publication of this "story of a conversion," Merton wrote that his motives for entering the Trappists were then strongly colored by negative feelings towards the world which he was leaving. The emphasis lay on the break with and the departure from the sinful, egocentric and money-hungry world. But since 1941 much had happened. He wrote in the preface:

> Since that time I have learned, I believe, to look back into that world with greater compassion, seeing those in it not as alien to myself, not as peculiar and deluded strangers, but as identified with myself. (p. 9)

In silence his flight from people had become compassion for them. And after years of prayer and contemplation he found people again at the bottom of his solitude, people upon whom he had turned his back. This insight made him not only a highly respected spiritual leader of the students of Gethsemani but also an engaged critic of the events from 1960-68, and one of the most outspoken proponents of nonviolence. Merton saw his monastery not only as a haven, where men sought to purify themselves so as to know God, but also as a center of spiritual action, from which he was to unmask the illusions of this world in a challenging way. The more he discovered the concrete demands of living, the less he emphasized living to purify himself.

> My monastery is not a home. It is not a place where I am rooted and established on the earth. It is not an environment in which I become aware of myself as an individual, but rather a place in which I disappear from the world as an object of interest in order to be everywhere in it by hiddenness and compassion. (Preface to the Japanese edition, p. 11)

But these words were written after 25 years of monastery life, and were the fruit of a long search, both in the depths of his own soul and in the many often-shocking events of his day. In this new dialogue with the world, he had not only seen the sense and the necessity of a close involvement with the actualities but also had experienced the real limitations of this.

In his book *Conjectures of a Guilty Bystander* he wrote:

> There is a time for action, a time for "commitment," but never for total involvement in the intricacies of a move-

ment. There is a moment of innocence and *kairos*, when action makes a great deal of sense. But who can recognize such moments? Not he who is debauched by a series of programs. And when all action has become absurd, shall one continue to act simply because once, a long time ago, it made a great deal of sense? As if one were always getting somewhere? There is a time to listen, in the active life as everywhere else, and the better part of action is waiting, not knowing what next, and not having a glib answer. (*CGB*, p. 156)

Merton himself had described the unrest of the civil rights fight as a *kairos*, a special time for the whites to pass over to action and to change their hearts. But he had also seen the powerlessness of a nonviolent resistance and the threatening rise of violence, and he had to admit that only his naked faith could give him hope when everything seemed dark.

The world about him looked like a desert. Merton lived in the midst of it but had the strength and power to remain true to the spirit of truth in himself. His belief in love and truth helped him to remain involved in the social and political misery. But there was more. John Eudes Bamberger, monk and psychiatrist, who was both Merton's student and physician in Gethsemani (and who for many years had been through much with him), wrote after Merton's death that one of the characteristics of Merton which made him both a fascinating and an irritating personality was his capricious manner of judgment. He could sometimes assert seemingly contradictory things about a situation, one after the other. He first called the monastery his favorite home, and later he asserted that it was in fact no place where he could be rooted and established. He called Rilke in one conference the most fantastic poet of this century, and a few weeks later in another conference he said: "He was awfully limited. . . . (*Continuum,* Vol. 7, No. 2, Summer 1969, p. 235)

Merton himself was conscious of this characteristic. In his introduction to *Seeds of Contemplation* he warned the reader not to stop with one strong statement, but allow it to be relativized by another strong statement, which he would find elsewhere. It was this dialectic which once in a while led Merton into difficulties. His fellow monks could not always understand him and the young monks whom he supervised were sometimes very confused by this feature of his teaching. When Merton on one day would assert exactly the opposite from the previous day, his listeners were irritated and said that they didn't know what he was worth.

This characteristic could suggest a cynicism which shunned every involvement by paralyzing a thought, an idea, or a suggestion by constantly asserting the opposite. Someone who constantly says at the very moment that he starts to become enthusiastic, "But you can also look at it from the other side," will never get moving and in place of a guilty bystander, will become a bitter cynic. But Merton did not become a cynic. When he saw how the American of his time was moved by greater violence and confusion, was completely missing the chance of reform and was threatening to land in a dangerous polarization of power, he did not turn away in bitterness and disappointment. Instead he went for advice more and more to the wise men from the East, for whom contradictions and paradoxes do not lead to bitterness but to truth. He sought from them a better understanding of the situation of the West. Therefore we now must turn to Merton's studies of the Chinese philosopher Chuang Tzu and Zen Buddhism, in order to see how he perceived the relation between Buddhism and Christianity.

The writer-philosopher Chuang Tzu had a very great influence on the thinking and feeling of Merton. He was one of the greatest Taoists during the flowering of Chinese philosophy, from 550 to 250 B.C., and his thinking and spirit exercise even today a deeply penetrating influence on the different Zen schools in China and Japan.

What did Merton learn from Chuang Tzu? Nothing. Merton learned from him what Suzuki had said about Zen: "Zen teaches nothing; it merely enables us to wake up and become aware. It does not teach, it points." (*Zen,* pp. 49-50) Merton added to this:

> The acts and gestures of a Zen Master are no more "statements" than is the ringing of an alarm clock. (*Zen,* pp. 49-50)

In this sense Chuang Tzu is a real master for Merton: he taught him nothing new but awakened and led him through the barrier of his own inner contradictions to the deeper ground of his consciousness. It is therefore understandable that Merton wrote about his book *The Way of Chuang Tzu:* ". . . I have enjoyed writing this book more than any other I can remember. . . . I simply like Chuang Tzu because he is what he is and I feel no need to justify this liking to myself or to anyone else" (*CT*, pp. 9-10). This is understandable because Chuang Tzu was, like Merton, a person who did not have to defend his own existence. Merton called Chuang Tzu a "subtle, funny, provoking thinker who doesn't easily put one over on you." John Eudes Bamberger says rightly that Chuang Tzu was a mirror-image of Merton and that Merton unconsciously identified in such a way with Chuang Tzu that a defense for his interest in Chuang Tzu seemed like a ridiculous self-defense.

The key to the thought of Chuang Tzu is then, at the same time, a key to understanding Merton himself. This seems abundantly clear when Merton describes this key as:

> . . . The complementarity of opposites, and this can be seen only when one grasps the central "pivot" of Tao which passes squarely through both "Yes" and "No," "I" and "Not-I." Life is a continual development. All beings are in a state of flux. Chuang Tzu would have agreed with Herakleitos. What is impossible today may suddenly become possible tomorrow. What is good and pleasant today may, tomorrow, become evil and odious. What seems right from one point of view may, when seen from a different aspect, manifest itself as completely wrong. (*CT*, p. 30)

These words are of great importance not only because Merton had experienced great contradictions in himself, not only because he had discovered in people and events that he studied the most dramatic contradictions, but especially because he himself had noticed that what is today a sensible reaction, tomorrow may better remain unspoken, and what in the beginning ap pears the proper way of action, later can do more evil than good. Precisely on the fast-developing social stage of the United States, Merton had found how so-called consistency and logic often lead to despairing absurdity. The temptation to hold fast to a once-chosen technique or form of action is all too great. Who can recognize the moment that the old solution becomes senseless? Not the one who has buried himself in strategies and techniques, nor the one who expects good to come from a method, whether this is now called nonviolence or revolution. If one does that, then one will go on with actions which have become absurd, just because they seemed fruitful once long ago. (See *CGB*, p. 156) These reflections forced Merton to go deeper than the level on which contradictions exist. He had seen that what is called good luck by one becomes bad luck for the other, that what is called justice here is called injustice 'there, and that what is sought by virtue and merit slips away at the moment that men think that they possess it. This experience forced him to ask: "Am I concerned then with conquering happiness, peace and justice? Am I concerned with joy, love, patience, and the rest as objects of my striving?" Chuang Tzu made him alert for these questions. Merton wrote:

Chuang Tzu . . . believes that the whole concept of "happiness" and "unhappiness" is ambiguous from the start, since it is situated in the world of objects. This is no less true of more refined concepts like virtue, justice, and so on. In fact, it is especially true of "good and evil," or "right and wrong." From the moment they are treated as "objects to be attained," these values lead to delusion and alienation. Therefore Chuang Tzu agrees with the paradox of Lao Tzu, "When all the world recognizes good as good, it becomes evil," because it becomes something that one does not have which one must constantly be pursuing until, in effect, it becomes unattainable. (*CT*, pp. 22-23)

Merton noted that Chuang Tzu who seldom worked with reasoning but spoke in pictures, said himself:

> . . . when the shoe fits
> The foot is forgotten,
> When the belt fits
> The belly is forgotten,
> When the heart is right
> "For" and "against" are forgotten. (*CT*, p. 112)

Merton is accused by many critics of being against technology and not valuing the great conquests of objective science. Especially after the publication of *Conjectures of a Guilty Bystander*, some were disappointed over Merton's relativizing of the great discoveries of modern humanity. His statements come, however, out of a very different source than one might think. He is not the monk who looks down with contempt on the busy, complicated, technical world and lives rather in the virgin nature. He is instead one who asks himself whether what we win with the right hand is not lost by the left. Merton had studied not only Chuang Tzu but also Levi-Strauss, the anthropologist and founder of structuralism. His ideas of the Western technological culture had also sparked Merton's interest in the question of whether the modern means by which we try to reach our ends really leads to human advancement. This question preoccupied him until his death. In his last diary he wrote: ". . . Today with a myriad of instruments we can explore things we never imagined. But we can no longer see directly what is right in front of us" (*CGB*, p. 281).

The core of this problem lies in Western man's tendency toward objectivizing and externalizing. Is it perhaps that the most valuable things that we want to gain with technology are already present within ourselves? Chuang Tzu expressed this in his own poetical manner:

> If a man steps on a stranger's foot
> In the marketplace,
> He makes a polite apology
> And offers an explanation
> ("This place is so terribly
> Crowded!").

> If an elder brother
> Steps on his younger brother's foot,
> He says, "Sorry!"
> And that is that.

> If a parent
> Treads on his child's foot,
> Nothing is said at all.

> The greatest politeness
> Is free of all formality.
> Perfect conduct
> Is free of concern.
> Perfect wisdom
> Is unplanned.
> Perfect love
> Is without demonstrations.
> Perfect sincerity offers
> No guarantee.   (*CT*, p. 138)

The thought that what is most holy permits no blind externalization or objectification gave Merton even more concern, since his life was a search for God. He wrote:

The more one seeks "the good" outside oneself as something to be acquired, the more one is faced with the necessity of discussing, studying, understanding, analyzing the nature of the good. The more, therefore, one becomes involved in abstractions and in the confusion of divergent opinions. The more "the good" is objectively analyzed, the more it is treated as something to be attained by special virtuous techniques, the less real it becomes. As it becomes less real, it recedes further into the distance of abstraction, futurity, unattainability. The more, therefore, one concentrates on the means to be used to attain it. And as the end becomes more remote and more difficult, the means become more elaborate and complex, until finally the mere study of the means becomes so demanding that all one's effort must be concentrated on this, and the end is forgotten. . . . This is, in fact, nothing but organized despair: "the good" that is preached and exacted by the moralist thus finally becomes evil, and all the more so since the hopeless pursuit of it distracts one from the real good which one already possesses and which one now despises or ignores. (*CT*, p. 23)

Everyone who studies theology must feel himself challenged by these words. The questions are unavoidable: Does all this talk and discussion about God bring us closer to him? Does our intelligent analysis and our detailed working out of the mystery of salvation bring us closer to the source of truth? Does the constantly greater emphasis on theology as an objective science open the way to him whom we seek? Or is it true, as Chuang Tzu said, that we have become blind to him whom we already possess, and that we try desperately with even more complicated means to get a hold on Him whom we seek, but who continually remains beyond our grasp. Merton said that this manner of relating to God was organized despair, which makes good into evil, God into Satan. Are we the kind of theologians who can only be happy when God is a problem? Chuang Tzu said:

If an expert does not have some problem to vex him,
    he is unhappy!
If a philosopher's teaching is never attacked,
    he pines away!
If critics have no one on whom to exercise their
    spite, they are unhappy.

All such men are prisoners in the world of
   objects. (*CT*, p. 141)

Is there no way out of this impasse? If there were no
exit, then Merton would have become a bitter man
who gave up upon noticing that a certain planned
strategy had no results. He had already heard from
Gandhi that nonviolence was more than a tactic, a
strategy or a technique, and demanded a nonviolent
heart that only could be formed in solitude by prayer
and fasting. Chuang Tzu who lived more than 2000
years before Gandhi, helped Merton further on this
path. He led him from nonviolence to non-action. And
it is just this non-action from Chuang Tzu that Merton
saw as a way out of our estrangement from God. He
wrote:

The secret of the way proposed by Chuang Tzu is . . . not
the accumulation of virtue and merit . . . but . . . the
non-doing, or non-action, which is not intent upon results
and is not concerned with consciously laid plans or deliberately organized endeavors: "My greatest happiness
consists precisely in doing nothing whatever that is calculated to obtain happiness. . . . Perfect joy is to be without joy. . . . If you ask 'what ought to be done' and 'what
ought not to be done' on earth to produce happiness, I
answer that these questions do not have a fixed and pre-
determined answer" to suit every case. If one is in harmony with Tao—the cosmic Tao, "Great Tao"—the answer
will make itself clear when the time comes to act, for
then one will act not according to the human and self-

conscious mode of deliberation, but according to the divine and spontaneous mode of *wu wei,* which is the mode of action of Tao itself, and is therefore the source of all good. (*CT,* p. 24)

For Merton this meant: the closer God is, the less means are necessary. Even words become superfluous in speaking with God. He who has no more words has found God. Chuang Tzu said:

> The purpose of a fish trap is to catch fish, and when the fish are caught, the trap is forgotten.
> The purpose of a rabbit snare is to catch rabbits. When the rabbits are caught, the snare is forgotten.
> The purpose of words is to convey ideas. When the ideas are grasped, the words are forgotten.
> Where can I find a man who has forgotten words? He is the one I would like to talk to. (*CT,* p. 154)

This non-action also holds for the contemplative life itself. It is striking to see how Merton relativized, towards the end of his life, the contemplation about which he had written so many books, booklets, articles and pamphlets. In a lecture he gave in October 1967, he said:

> . . . I would say that it is very important in the contemplative life not to over-emphasize the contemplation. If we're always thinking about contemplation, contemplation, contemplation, union with God, mystical union and intimate experiences with God, etc., that's fine, that's all very well. But if we constantly over-emphasize those

things to which access is inevitably something quite rare, we overlook the ordinary authentic real experiences of everyday life as real things to enjoy, things to be happy about, things to praise God for.

("Is the Contemplative Life Finished?" Notes from a taped conference. Oct. 1967, p. 24 or *CWA*, p. 351)

Perhaps Merton had experienced even more the artificiality of the distinction between contemplation and action. Chuang Tzu had showed him this sharply. Merton wrote:

A contemplative and interior life which would simply make the subject more aware of himself and permit him to become obsessed with his own interior progress would, for Chuang Tzu, be no less an illusion than the active life of the "benevolent" man who would try by his own efforts to impose his idea of the good on those who might oppose this idea—and thus in his eyes, become "enemies of the good." The true tranquility sought by the "man of Tao" is *Ying ning*, tranquility in the action of non-action, in other words, a tranquility which transcends the division between activity and contemplation by entering into union with the nameless and invisible Tao. (*CT*, p. 26)

Chuang Tzu said this as follows:

> Fishes are born in water
> Man is born in Tao.
> If fishes, born in water,
> Seek the deep shadow
> of pond and pool,

All their needs
Are satisfied.

If man, born in Tao,
Sinks into the deep shadow
Of non-action
To forget aggression and concern,
He lacks nothing
His life is secure.

Moral: "All the fish needs
Is to get lost in water.
All man needs is to get lost
In Tao." (*CT*, p. 65)

Seen in this way, non-action means not only avoiding goal-oriented plans and strategies in order to find happiness "somewhere outside," but also avoiding introverted self-analysis. Non-action (which does not stand in contrast to activism) is a consequence of the experience that God is not an óbject that can be conquered as a possession, but is the *all*, in which we can lose ourselves.

And in this experience all the old has become new, without essentially changing, since the contradiction between old and new had also fallen away. From this comes the Zen-saying:

... Before I grasped Zen, the mountains were nothing but mountains and the rivers nothing but rivers. When I got into Zen, the mountains were no longer mountains and the rivers no longer rivers. But when I understood Zen, the mountains were only mountains and the rivers only rivers. (*Zen*, p. 140)

There still remains the question: What can the East teach the West? The answer from the East is once again: nothing. The East can only awaken what has fallen asleep in the Western consciousness. Chuang Tzu said nothing that had not already been heard by Merton within the Christian tradition. Nevertheless Buddhism kept him intensely preoccupied, especially after the meeting with Daisetz Suzuki. This meeting made a deep impression on Merton:

> . . . In meeting him one seemed to meet that "True Man of No Title" that Chuang Tzu and the Zen Masters speak of. . . . In meeting Dr. Suzuki and drinking a cup of tea with him I felt I had met this one man. It was like finally arriving at one's own home. (*Zen*, p. 61)

Merton who already earlier had studied Buddhism and often was confused by the many mysterious words, images, legends and rites, was freed from this by Suzuki.

The most important of Merton's studies of Zen Buddhism are *Mystics and Zen Masters* and *Zen and the Birds of Appetite*. The first is composed especially of descriptive studies, in which Merton tries to give as clear a picture as possible of what Zen-Buddhism is, and the second directs itself especially to the dialogue with Christianity. It is appropriate that we end our study with a few remarks on *Zen and the Birds of Appetite*, published in 1968, in order to better appreciate the last phase of Merton's life and thought, which led him to Bangkok where he died.

When Merton asked himself where precisely the East can open the eyes of the West, he returned continually to the meaning of *kenosis*, the self-emptying which holds such a great place in both the Eastern and the Western mystical traditions, but which in the West, unfortunately, is largely lost through the dubious glorification of the "ego." The feeling of self-importance of activity-oriented Westerners depends greatly upon the question of what they can achieve, or what power and influence they have. They judge their fellow beings according to what they possess, how much they produce, how much money they earn and how many contacts they have. Such persons have put the *self* in the center of their thought. For the Westerner, Merton said:

> . . . The concept of the self as a clearly present, very con-
> crete center of decision has considerable importance. It
> matters very much what you are thinking, saying, doing,
> deciding, here and now. It matters very much what your
> current commitments are, whom you are with, whom you
> are against, where you claim to be going, what button you
> wear, whom you vote for—all this is important. This is
> obviously proper to men of action who feel that there are
> old structures to be torn down and new ones to be built.
> But from such men we must not yet expect either patience
> with or understanding of mysticism. (*Zen*, p. 29)

We modern Westerners are so busy with ourselves, so preoccupied with the question of whether we do justice to our own selves, that the experience of the "transcendent" becomes practically impossible. In the way of thinking which involves talking, discussing, analyzing and criticizing, in which one opinion asks the other for attention, in which belief is replaced more and more by an endless list of conceptions, opinions, visions and ideas which whirl around as paper boats on the sea—in this way of thinking there is scarcely room for Him who speaks whenever we are silent and who comes in whenever we have emptied ourselves. Instead of making ourselves susceptible to the experience of the transcendent God, we, busy about many things, begin to seek after the small flighty sensations brought about by artificial stimulation of the senses. Also Merton recognized this danger of glorifying the ego even within the contemplative life itself. He noted:

> . . . It becomes overwhelmingly important for us to become detached from our everyday conception of ourselves as potential subjects for special and unique experience, or as candidates for realization, attainment and fulfillment . . . this means that a spiritual guide worth his salt will conduct a ruthless campaign against all forms of delusion arising out of spiritual ambition and self-complacency which aim to establish the ego in spiritual glory. That is why a St. John of the Cross is so hostile to visions, ecstacies and all forms of "special experience." That is why the Zen Masters say: "If you meet the Buddha, kill him." (*Zen*, p. 76-77)

Merton hopes that perhaps the East could help us again recognize the Christian sense of *kenosis,* self-emptying. The actual experience of God will never really be possible if we are constantly busy with the cultivation of our own personalities by a spurious spirituality. The Zen-Buddhist can point out to the Christian the possibility of self-emptying and searching for a direct and pure experience of the transcendent, freed from all self-preoccupation. To the extent that we deemphasize our "self," the need to understand God in verbal formulas and linguistic constructions also disappears. Merton hoped that whenever the Christian has the courage to renounce this concern with self he would also find the actual meaning of the Christian experience of God:

> . . . All transcendent experience is for the Christian a participation in "the mind of Christ"—"Let this mind be in you which was also in Christ Jesus . . . who *emptied* himself . . . obedient unto death. . . . Therefore God raised him and conferred upon him a name above all names." (Phil 2:5-10). This dynamic of emptying and of transcendence accurately defines the transformation of the Christian consciousness in Christ. It is a kenotic transformation, an emptying of all the contents of the ego-consciousness to become a void in which the light of God or the glory of God, the full radiation of the infinite reality of His Being and Love are manifested. (*Zen,* p. 75)

Just as the black must bring the white to conversion, so must the East make the West Christian again. With this conviction Merton went to the East. On the 10th of December, 1968, in Bangkok, a few hours after his lecture on Marxism and the monastic ideal, he met death by electrocution when he came into contact with a faulty electric fan.

The U.S.A. Army officials in Bangkok provided the embalming and coffin, and flew his body in a U.S. Army plane back to Kentucky. Seeing the irony of this, former abbot Dom James Fox remarked: "True enough, I'll wager he had a good laugh in Heaven at all this." (Letter by Dom James Fox about Merton's death, p. 5.)

Part II
FOR MEDITATION

ACKNOWLEDGMENTS

Acknowledgment is made to the following publishers for permission to reprint excerpts from the writings of Thomas Merton.

From THE SIGN OF JONAS, copyright 1953, by The Abbey of Our Lady of Gethsemani. Reprinted by permission of Harcourt Brace Jovanovich, Inc.

From MY ARGUMENT WITH THE GESTAPO, copyright 1969, by The Abbey of Gethsemani, Inc. Copyright 1968 by Thomas Merton. Reprinted by permission of Doubleday & Company, Inc.

From FAITH AND VIOLENCE. Reprinted by permission of the University of Notre Dame Press.

From THOUGHTS IN SOLITUDE, copyright 1956, 1958 by The Abbey of Our Lady of Gethsemani. From THE SECULAR JOURNAL OF THOMAS MERTON, copyright 1959 by Madonna House. From SEEDS OF DESTRUCTION, copyright 1961, 1962, 1963, 1964 by The Abbey of Gethsemani. Reprinted with the permission of Farrar, Straus & Giroux, Inc.

From THE WAY OF CHUANG TZU, copyright 1965 by The Abbey of Gethsemani, Inc. From ZEN AND THE BIRDS OF APPETITE, copyright 1968 by The Abbey of Gethsemani, Inc. From GANDHI ON NONVIOLENCE, copyright 1964, 1965, by New Directions Publishing Corporation. Reprinted with the permission of New Directions Publishing Corporation, New York.

CHAPTER 6

From Sarcasm to Contemplation

SECULAR JOURNAL

October 1, 1939–November 27, 1941

Preface

Certainly the views and aspirations expressed, at times, with such dogmatic severity, have come to be softened and tempered with the passage of time and with a more intimate contact with the spiritual problems of other people. I hope I may be forgiven for having allowed some of my youthful sarcasms to survive in these pages. (viii-ix)

1. PERRY STREET—NEW YORK

February 18, 1940

There is a new biography of Joyce out which has confirmed what everybody probably suspected: that his personal life has been dreary and rather uninteresting. . . .

Joyce certainly looks like an Irishman who resisted a vocation to the priesthood, but he also looks more like a bookkeeper than a writer. That he happens to be the best writer in this century is quite apart from this, and nobody ever said that his looks had anything much to do with what he wrote. It is too bad he made the same mistake that the people who hate him have always made: that of making no distinction whatever between the culture of the Irish middle-class and the sacramental life of the Church. (pp. 27-8)

2. CUBA

April 18, 1940

Our modern rat-race civilization, having lost, at the same time, its respect for virginity and for fruitfulness, has replaced the virtue of chastity with a kind of hypochondriac reverence for perfect, sterile cleanliness: everything has to be wrapped in cellophane. Your reefers come to you untouched by human hands. Fruitfulness has lost its meaning but has degenerated into a kind of sentimental and idolatrous worship of sensation for its own sake that is so dull it makes you vomit: the fat blondes in the dirty picture magazines are getting bigger and fatter and more rubbery, and all the people who think they are so lusty are really worshiping frustration and barrenness. No wonder they go nuts and jump out of windows all the time. Such contradictions are completely unbearable, and cannot be replaced by a lot of mental and sexual gymnastics, the way the mental cripples who have been psychoanalyzed seem humbly to believe. (p. 88)

3. NEW YORK AND ST. BONAVENTURE

May 21, 1940

It is said that while the Germans were desecrating a church somewhere in Poland, some German sergeant, cockeyed with the excitement, stood up in front of the altar and yelled out that if there was a God He would want to prove His existence at once by striking down such a bold and important and terrifying fellow as this sergeant. God did not strike him down. The sergeant went away still excited, and probably the unhappiest man in the world: God had not acted like a Nazi. God was not, in fact, a Nazi, and God's justice (which everybody obscurely knows about in his bones, no matter what he tries to say he thinks) is inexpressibly different from the petty bloodthirsty revenge of Nazis. (p. 99)

June 16, 1940

The valley is full of oil storage tanks, and oil is for feeding bombers, and once they are fed they have to bomb something, and they generally pick on oil tanks.

Wherever you have oil tanks, or factories, or railroads or any of the comforts of home and manifestations of progress, in this century, you are sure to get bombers, sooner or later.

Therefore, if I don't pretend, like other people, to understand the war, I do know this much: that the knowledge of what is going on only makes it seem desperately important to be voluntarily poor, to get rid of all possessions this instant. I am scared, sometimes, to own anything, even a name, let alone coin, or shares in the oil, the munitions, the airplane factories. I am scared to take a proprietary interest in anything, for fear that my love of what I own may be killing somebody somewhere. (pp. 110-11)

May 30, 1940

Instead of having faith, which is a virtue, and therefore nourishes the soul and gives it a healthy life, people merely have a lot of opinions, which excite the soul but don't give it anything to feed it, just wear it out until it falls over from exhaustion. . . .

In this situation, where there are hundreds of people with no real faith, who don't really believe anything much, long inquiries are constantly being carried out as to what various persons "believe." Scientists, advertising men, sociologists, soldiers, critics, are all asked what they believe inasmuch as they are scientists, advertising men, etc. Apparently there is a separate belief appropriate to every walk of life. Anyway, they all answer with brisk one thousand word articles stating some opinion or other that they have picked up somewhere. The result is enough to make you break down and sob. (pp. 116-17)

June 25, 1940

We have no peace because we have done nothing to keep peace, not even prayed for it! We have not even *desired* peace except for the wrong reasons: because we didn't want to get hurt, we didn't want to suffer. But if the best reason we have for desiring peace is only that we are cowards, then we are lost from the start, because the enemy only sees in our cowardice his first and most effective weapon.

If we are ever going to have peace again, we will have to hate war for some better reason than that we fear to lose our houses, our refrigerators, our cars, our legs, our lives. If we are ever to get peace, we have got to desire something more than reefers and anesthetics. That is all we seem to want: anything to avoid pain. (pp. 121-22)

January 2, 1941

And so this is the New Year, 1941. I tried to tell myself a year of terrors, but the sun was out. It may well be, just the same. I am the worst of prophets: prophecy is the one thing, besides mathematics and being a soldier, that I am certain I have no gift for. Being an ice-man I am not certain about, never having tried. (pp. 147-48)

February 22, 1941

If I pray for peace, that prayer is only justified if it means one thing: not that the war may end, the fighting stop, and murdering and injustice continue some other way. To pray merely for the war to stop, and some fake armistice to be signed is not to pray for peace.

If I pray for peace, abstractly speaking it makes sense if I pray for a "just peace," although I do not know what, in political terms, would constitute a just peace now, and I am totally unable to get any relevance, politically, out of the term.

But when I pray for peace I pray for the following miracle. That God move all men to pray and do penance and recognize each one his own great guilt, because we are all guilty of this war, in a way. Bloy says somewhere, of a murderer, that all the people were a tree of which this murderer was only one of the fruits, and that applies to Hitler: we are a tree, of which he is one of the fruits, and we all nourish him, and he thrives most of all on our hatred and condemnation of him, when that condemnation disregards our own guilt, and piles the responsibility for everything upon somebody else's sins! (pp. 164-65)

4. INTERLUDE: ABBEY OF OUR LADY OF GETHSEMANI

April 7, 1941

I should tear out all the other pages of this book, and all the other pages of anything else I have ever written, and begin here.

This is the center of America. I had wondered what was holding the country together, what has been keeping the universe from cracking in pieces and falling apart. It is places like this monastery—not only this one: there must be others. . . .

This is the only real city in America—and it is by itself, in the wilderness. (p. 183)

April 8, 1941

. . . The religious life exists and thrives not in buildings or dead things or flowers or beasts but in the soul. And there it exists not as a "good feeling" but as a constant purpose, an unending love that expresses itself now as patience, now as humility, now as courage, now as self-denial, now as justice, but always in a strong knot of faith and hope, and all of these are nothing but aspects of one constant deep desire, charity, love. (p. 190)

April 10, 1941

We must long to learn the secret of our own nothingness (not God's secret first of all, but our own secret). But God alone can show us our own secret. Once we see it, we can seek to receive His love into our hearts, and we can desire to become like Him. Indeed, by His love we can begin to become like ourselves—that is we can find our own true selves, for we are made in His image and likeness.

God teaches us in tribulations. The most unfortunate people in the world are those who know no tribulations. The most unhappy men are really the ones who are able to bribe their way out of suffering and tribulation, and to evade the issue, in pleasures, in wars, in devotion to a cause like Nazism—which is moral suicide. (p. 197)

April 12, 1941

. . . I wonder if I have learned enough to pray for humility. I desire only one thing: to love God. Those who love Him, keep His commandments. I only desire to do one thing: to follow His will. I pray that I am at least beginning to know what that may mean. Could it ever possibly mean that I might some day become a monk in this monastery? My Lord, and my King, and my God! (p. 203)

5. ST. BONAVENTURE, HARLEM, AND OUR LADY OF THE VALLEY

May 19, 1941

I am amazed at all the novels I read between the ages of seventeen and twenty. I was never able to swallow Hardy, although I read practically everything else, D. H. Lawrence, Stella Benson, Virginia Woolf, John Dos Passos, Jules Romains, Hemingway, Balzac, Flaubert, Celine, even some short stories by Stefan Zweig, some Vicki Baum, and the other day when I was sitting in the sun I remembered with embarrassment how I tried to explain to my godfather why I liked Luciano Zuccoli's bad pornographic novel *La Divina Fanciulla*. I said it was "very Italian."

I have read enough novels, and I don't want to read any more. Also, I think the novel is a lousy art form anyway. (pp. 218-19)

May 23, 1941

I was never so convinced of anything as that I haven't any idea what this is all about, what people are doing. I think a lot of people are crazy, and a lot of people just refuse to have anything happen to them, and have become, instinctively, stubborn, in a fairly good, animal sort of way. They won't be moved. (p. 222)

August 15, 1941

While I was saying prayers in St. Patrick's Cathedral, I saw Harlem standing afar off like the publican . . . who did not even dare look up to heaven!

Then gentle, ragged kids are running fast through the dark warrens of the tenements and out into the street. A mother cries out to one of them: "Don't fly your kite on the roof! Don't go up there to fly your kite. It will drag you away!"

The other day I went to the Baroness' place for the first time. . . . They [young Negroes] were sitting around a table having an argument about something. It went like this: One would say, "Well I don't think that's right," and everybody would burst out laughing. Then another would say, "Well I *do* think that's right," and they would all burst out laughing again. They were very happy, and it didn't matter much what they were arguing about. I'm sure that's the best kind of argument to have, anyway, happy. (pp. 236-37)

September 3, 1941

The measure of our identity, or our being (for here the two mean exactly the same thing) is the amount of our love for God. The more we love earthly things, reputation, importance, ease, success and pleasures, for ourselves, the less we love God. Our identity gets dissipated among a lot of things that do not have the value we imagine we see in them, and we are lost in them: we know it obscurely by the way all these things disappoint us and sicken us once we get what we have desired. Yet we still bring ourselves to nothing, annihilate our lives by trying to fulfill them on things that are incapable of doing so. When we really come to die, at last, we suddenly know how much we have squandered and thrown away, and we see that we are truly annihilated by our own sick desires: we were nothing, but everything God gave us we have also reduced to nothing, and now we are pure death. (pp. 243-44)

November 6, 1941

No need for anything new, or for any excitement whatever. If I pray, either I will change my mind or I will not [whether to go to work in Harlem or not]. In any case, God will guide me. No need to be up in arms, no need to be anything other than what I am—but I will pray and fast harder. No more excitements, arguments, tearing of hair, trips to Cuba and grandiose "farewell world" gestures. No need for anything special—special joy or special sorrow, special excitement or special torment. Everything is indifferent, except prayer, fasting, meditation—and work. I thank God and all the saints that I am not running around in circles—not yet. Defend me later, O God, against all scruples! (p. 216)

November 27, 1941

Today I think: should I be going to Harlem, or to the Trappists? Why doesn't this idea of the Trappists leave me? . . . But perhaps what I am afraid of is to write and be rejected. . . .

Would I not be obliged to admit, now, that if there is a choice for me between Harlem and the Trappists, I would not hesitate to take the Trappists? Is that why I hesitate to find out if the choice exists? . . .

Perhaps I cling to my independence, to the chance to write, to go where I like in the world. . . . It seems monstrous at the moment that I should consider my writing important enough even to enter the question. If God wants me to write, I can write anywhere. . . .

Going to live in Harlem does not seem to me to be anything special. It is a good and reasonable way to follow Christ. But going to the Trappists is exciting, it fills me with awe and desire. I return to the idea again and again: "Give up *everything*, give up *everything!*" (pp. 269-70)

CHAPTER 7

The Way to Silence

MY ARGUMENT WITH THE GESTAPO

This novel is a kind of sardonic meditation on the world in which I then found myself: an attempt to define its predicament and my own place in it. (p. 6)

DIALOGUE 1: Merton has come to England in 1941 from America to write a personal journal about the war. He meets a woman whom he knew years before.

B: I cannot understand you any more. You talk in a way I have forgotten how to understand. Understanding no longer means the same thing to both of us. If that is the way you have come here to interpret the war, it would have been better if you had stayed away.

M: I am not looking for the easy level on which it seems to be comprehensible and really is not.

B: The level of the fighters?

M: Yes. The opinions of politicians and soldiers have no meaning for me. But there must be other meanings, on another level, and I have come to look for them. (p. 28)

DIALOGUE 2: With two uniformed men who spied Merton sitting behind his typewriter near the window on the second floor of one of the bombed houses of London. They ask him who he is.

M: I am a writer. I write what I see out of the window. I am writing about the fear on the faces of the houses. I say as fast as I can, what preoccupation I see in the sick houses of bombarded London, and I write that the houses of bombarded London do not understand their own fear. . . .

First man: What have you just written about us? Have you written about our courage?

M: I have written that you folded your arms and frowned at me from under the shadows of your helmets. I have not written about your courage.

Second man: Who are you working for? Why do you write that our houses do not understand their fear: rather write that they do not understand their courage.

M: It is the same thing.

Second man: Then what do you know about our courage and our fear? Where do you come from? What is the basis of your statements about us? You say you write what you see, no two men see

the same street, here. What do you see that you
write? What do you mean when you talk about
our courage and our fear?

M: I am still trying to find out: and that is why I write.

Second man: How will you find out by writing?

M: I will keep putting things down until they become
clear.

Second man: And if they do not become clear?

M: I will have a hundred books, full of symbols, full of
everything I ever knew or ever saw or ever
thought.

Second man: If it never becomes clear, perhaps you
will have more books than if it were all clear at
once.

M: No doubt. But I say if it were all clear at once, I
would not really understand it, either. Some
things are too clear to be understood, and what
you think is your understanding of them is only
a kind of charm, a kind of incantation in your
mind concerning that thing. This is not understanding: it is something you remember. So
much for definition! We always have to go back
and start from the beginning and make over all
the definitions for ourselves again. (pp. 52-53)

First man: Then do you know what our courage consists in?

M: No.

First man: What does it mean to you, then?

M: Very little. I cannot understand why the men that
came in black hundreds out of the hotels and

onto the dunes of Dunkerque and staggered into the sea where rowboats were waiting to take them in twos and threes to England, I cannot understand why these men did not go mad with the songs that ran over and over in the same broken grooves of their minds, during that escape.

I do not understand those soldiers, blind with weariness and confusion and weakness, wading away from the fires among the dunes, with nothing in their heads but: "Oh Johnny, Oh Johnny, how you can love. Oh Johnny, Oh Johnny, Oh Johnny," until the low-flying Messerschmitts got them with their machine guns.

I do not understand the thousand sailors of the sinking *Hood*, drowned in the Iceland sea with the saddest and craziest and lousiest songs that were ever written in the history of the world rolling over and over in the barrels of their heads.

Do not ask me to explain the fleeing soldiers who were found shot to pieces with their packs full of impossible pictures of big rubber women all legs and breasts and red underwear and big, white grinning heads.

I do not understand any of the things they lived by, or seem to have died for: these songs, these pictures, and all the interminable series of limericks that they recited over and over every spare moment of their lives. I do not understand the fabulous courage of soldiers and sailors, dying with their minds full of such weird and ugly lumber, and I do not even know if it is courage. (pp. 55-56)

DIALOGUE 3: With B.

M: I cannot argue about the war, or anything else. I do not like it. I wish it were over. Whoever wins, it is going to be very hard. I have no ideas about justice, who is right, who is wrong. I know that a lot of people are being killed.

B: Don't you believe the Germans started the war?

M: In the sense that they began fighting it, yes.

B: Germany is guilty.

M: I don't know the meaning of the word guilty, except in the sense that I also am guilty for the war, partly.

B: You? Now I don't understand you.

M: I don't understand you, either. I cannot use the word guilty in a sentence like "Germany is guilty," because I don't understand the level of meanings on which the word works, in that application. I understand it differently.

B: How could you be guilty of a war? Nations are guilty of wars.

M. Nations don't exist. They can't be held responsible for anything. Nations are made up of people, and people are responsible for the things they do. I am a person: I can be guilty of wrong, I can do harm, and have done.

B: They say Hitler is guilty.

M: He might be. Only I don't know enough about it. He might be more guilty than any other one person, but he isn't the only person guilty of the war, and as to saying how guilty he is, I'm afraid I don't know, I don't know. I don't know who's guilty All I know is, if anything happens to the world, it is partly because of me. That is all I know: my share in it. But I don't even know the relation of my share to all the rest of the responsibilities, and don't attempt to.

B: I haven't time to know as little as you want to know.

M: It doesn't take time.

B: It takes getting used to.

M: It depends how much you want to get used to it.

B: I don't at all. I stay up all night, I hang on to the walls and the explosions of bombs break my back in half, I live in black smoke of this city's burning, and the dust of the ruins is always in my throat. I don't want to know that nobody's responsible. I want to know that one man is. I haven't time to know anything less arbitrary than that. Tomorrow I may be dead.

M: What difference will it make, then, what political fact you happen to have known?

B: I want to know who is responsible.

M: Even if it isn't really true?

B: In the simple sense in which I want to know it, it will be true enough for me: I will have been killed by one of their bombers, and the symbol on the rudder will be enough for a judgment.

M: You want to die, perfectly sure of who it is you hate?

B: Yes, why not? At least it is something definite to die with.

M: Not definite enough for me, and not the kind of definiteness I want. I want to die knowing something besides double-talk.

B: There is no such thing as double-talk, not to me, there isn't. Not any more.

B: (a little later) Is that what you are here to find out? Your part in what is happening? Do you want to know how much you yourself are responsible for?

M: You guessed it. (pp. 76-78)

DIALOGUE 4: With candles on the altar.

C: You who went away from here [England] lost, would you ever have returned here if you had been lost still?

M: I make this journey for the reasons Dante made his.

C: Are you an exile, stranger?

M: Yes, I am an exile all over the earth.

C: You who have wanted to return to the midst of this fire and penance, for Dante's reasons, are you afraid that you are in danger, in this hostile country?

M: I know I am in danger, but how can I be afraid of danger? If I remember I am nothing, I will know the danger can take nothing from me.

C: And yet, are you afraid of the danger?

M: Yes, I am afraid, because I forget that I am nothing. If I remembered that I have nothing called my own that will not be lost anyway, that only what is not mine but God's will ever live, then I would not fear so many false fears. (pp. 137-38)

CHAPTER 8

Conquering Solitude

THE SIGN OF JONAS

December 10, 1946–July 4, 1952

Prologue

. . . For me, the vow of stability has been the belly of the whale. I have always felt a great attraction to the life of perfect solitude. It is an attraction I shall probably never entirely lose. During my years as a student at Gethsemani, I often wondered if this attraction was not a genuine vocation to some other religious Order. . . . My own solution of this problem is the main theme of the present book. Like the prophet Jonas, whom God ordered to go to Nineveh, I found myself with an almost uncontrollable desire to go in the opposite direction. God pointed one way and all my "ideals" pointed in the other. It was when Jonas was traveling as fast as he could away from Nineveh, toward Tharsis, that he was thrown overboard, and swallowed by a whale who took him where God wanted him to go. . . . Like Jonas himself I find myself traveling toward my destiny in the belly of a paradox. (pp. 20-21)

PART ONE: SOLEMN PROFESSION

December 13, 1946

. . . Jay Laughlin wants two anthologies for New Directions press. I wonder if I will ever be able to do them. If God wills. Meanwhile, for myself, I have only one desire and that is the desire for solitude—to disappear into God, to be submerged in His peace, to be lost in the secret of His Face. (p. 26)

December 24, 1946

. . . I was in Father Abbot's room complaining that I was not the contemplative or the solitary that I wanted to be, that I made no progress in this house and that I ought to be either a Carthusian or an outright hermit. . . . (p. 27)

February 18, 1947

If Jesus wants me to be here at Gethsemani, as my Superiors insist He does (*Qui vos audit me audit*), then perhaps He does not want me to be a pure contemplative after all. I suppose it all depends what you mean by a pure contemplative. (p. 33)

February 20, 1947

Went and talked over the whole business of my vocation again with Father Abbot and he assured me once again, patiently, that everything was quite all right and this was where I belonged. In my bones I know that he is quite right and that I am a fool. And yet, on the surface, everything seems to be all wrong. As usual, I am making too much fuss about it. (p. 34)

March 11, 1947

However, the important thing is not to live for contemplation but to live for God. That is obvious, because, after all, that is the contemplative vocation. (p. 38)

April 3, 1947

Once again, it seems to me that I ought to give up all desire for the lights and satisfactions that make me too pleased with myself at prayer. I should want nothing but to do all the ordinary things a monk has to do, regularly and properly, without any special thought of satisfaction in them. (p. 44)

May 4, 1947

I will no longer wound myself with the thoughts and questions that have surrounded me like thorns: that is a penance You do not ask of me.

You have made my soul for Your peace and Your silence, but it is lacerated by the noise of my activity and my desires. My mind is crucified all day by its own hunger for experience, for ideas, for satisfaction. And I do not possess my house in silence. . . .

I am content that these pages show me to be what I am—noisy, full of the racket of my imperfections and passions, and the wide open wounds left by my sins. Full of my own emptiness. Yet, ruined as my house is, You live there! (p. 54)

June 13, 1947

Today I seemed to be very much assured that solitude is indeed His will for me and that it is truly God Who is calling me into the desert. But this desert is not necessarily a geographical one. It is a solitude of heart in which created joys are consumed and reborn in God. (p. 59)

August 15, 1947

No matter how much I might *like* to be a Carthusian or something else, I could never make a move to become one unless I had some positive indication that it was the will of God. And I have no such indication. Even when I try to pry some expression of approval or encouragement out of my director I find myself with a hole in my conscience that tells me clearly there is something wrong. (p. 68)

October 12, 1947

What is the use of my complaining about not being a contemplative, if I do not take the opportunities I get for contemplation? I suppose I take them, but in the wrong way. I spend the time looking for something to read about contemplation—something to satisfy my raffish spiritual appetite—instead of shutting up and emptying my mind and leaving the inner door open for the Holy Spirit to enter from the inside, all the doors being barred and all my blinds down. (p. 76)

PART TWO: DEATH OF AN ABBOT

September 12, 1948

Here is what you need to do more and more—shut up about all that—architecture, Spirit of the Order, contemplation, liturgy, chant—be simple and poor or you will never have any peace. Take what is atrocious without complaint, unless you are in some way officially bound to complain. Otherwise keep still. But if everything really gets awful? . . . (pp. 122-23)

September 20, 1948

I know why I will never really be able to write anything about prayer in a journal—because anything you write, even a journal, is at least implicitly somebody else's business. When I say prayer I mean what happens to me in the first person singular. What really happens to what is really me is nobody else's business. (p. 124)

PART THREE: MAJOR ORDERS

December 1, 1948

During the past year—temptations to become a Carthusian have more or less subsided. It seems to me they began to subside the precise moment when, on retreat last year, I opened an envelope from France which had a thirteenth-century picture of Saint Louis in it, from Father Anselme Dimier, at Tamié. Dom Marie Joseph helped and Dom Gabriel helped and I am ashamed to say the success of *The Seven Storey Mountain* helped and Dom James got me to declare formally that I didn't intend to run off and be a Carthusian, before he would let me be a sub-deacon. (p. 139)

April 6, 1949

. . . I find myself accepting the idea that perhaps I do not have a purely contemplative vocation. I say "accept." I do not *believe* it. It is utterly impossible for me to believe any such thing: everything in me cries out for solitude and for God alone. And yet I find myself admitting that perhaps I don't know what that really means, and that I am too low in the spiritual scale of things to grasp it, and even that I am somehow excluded from it by God's love. The feeling is absolutely terrible—the power of attraction that seems to draw the whole life out of me, to tear out the roots of my soul— and then the blank wall against which I stop—dead. (pp. 175-76)

PART FOUR: TO THE ALTAR OF GOD

May 24, 1949

Also: in my prayer and all my interior life, such as it is, I am concerned with the need for a greater and more complete interior silence: an interior secrecy that amounts to not even thinking about myself. Silence about my prayer, about the development of my interior life, is becoming an absolute necessity, so that I am beginning to believe I should stop writing about contemplation altogether, except perhaps in the most general terms. It seems to me to be a great indecency for me to pass, in the opinion of men, as one who seems to have something to say about contemplation. The thought makes me feel as if I needed a bath and a change of clothing. (pp. 189-90)

June 4, 1949

One of the most impressive people I have ever seen is Archbishop Paul Yu-Pin, of Nanking, who was here for the centenary. In fact, he spoke in Chapter about China and the contemplative life and Buddhist monasticism— and about the reproach that Buddhists fling at us, that is, we are all very fine at building hospitals but we have no contemplatives. He spoke of the two million (or was it five million?) Buddhist monks and nuns in China. . . . (p. 195)

July 21, 1949

I am finding myself forced to admit that my lamentations about my writing job have been foolish. At the moment, the writing is one thing that gives me access to some real silence and solitude. Also I find that it helps me to pray, because when I pause at my work I find that the mirror inside me is surprisingly clean and deep and serene and God shines there and is immediately found, without hunting, as if He had come close to me while I was writing and I had not observed His coming. And this, I think, should be the cause of great joy, and to me it is. (pp. 204-5)

August 8, 1949

By the reading of Scripture I am so renewed that all nature seems renewed around me and with me. The sky seems to be a pure, a cooler blue, the trees a deeper green, light is sharper on the outlines of the forest and the hills and the whole world is charged with the glory of God and I feel fire and music in the earth under my feet. (p. 212)

August 31, 1949

It does no good to use big words to talk about Christ. Since I seem to be incapable of talking about Him in the language of a child, I have reached the point where I can scarcely talk about Him at all. All my words fill me with shame. (p. 222)

PART FIVE: THE WHALE AND THE IVY

September 1, 1949

If I am to be a saint—and there is nothing else that I can think of desiring to be—it seems that I must get there by writing books in a Trappist monastery. If I am to be a saint, I have not only to be a monk, which is what all monks must do to become saints, but I must also put down on paper what I have become. It may sound simple, but it is not an easy vocation.

To be as good a monk as I can, and to remain myself, and to write about it: to put myself down on paper, in such a situation, with the most complete simplicity and integrity, masking nothing, confusing no issues: this is very hard, because I am all mixed up in illusions and attachments. These, too, will have to be put down. But without exaggeration, repetition, useless emphasis. No need for breast-beating and lamentation before the eyes of anyone but You, O God, who see the depths of my fatuity. To be frank without being boring. It is a kind of crucifixion. Not a very dramatic or painful one. But it requires so much honesty that it is beyond my nature. It must come somehow from the Holy Ghost. (pp. 228-29)

(From the introduction to part five)

And now, for the first time, I began to know what it means to be *alone*. Before becoming a priest I had made a great fuss about solitude and had been rather a nuisance to my superiors and directors in my aspirations for a solitary life. Now, after my ordination, I discovered that the essence of a solitary vocation is that it is a vocation to fear, to helplessness, to isolation in the invisible God. Having found this, I now began for the first time in my life to taste a happiness that was so complete and so profound that I no longer needed to reflect upon it. There was no longer any need to remind myself that I was happy—a vain expedient to prolong a transient joy—for this happiness was real and permanent and even in a sense eternal. It penetrated to the depths below consciousness, and in all storms, in all fears, in the deepest darkness, it was always unchangeably there. (p. 227)

December 15, 1949

. . . Working in the woods in the afternoon, I felt lonely and small and humiliated—chopping down dead trees with a feeling that perhaps I was not even a real person any more. . . .

Otherwise—feeling of fear, dejection, nonexistence. Yet it gives me a kind of satisfaction to realize that it is not by contact with any other creature that I can recover the sense that I am real. Solitude means being lonely not in a way that pleases you but in a way that frightens and empties you to the extent that it means being exiled even from yourself. (p. 243)

December 22, 1949

It is fear that is driving me into solitude. Love has put drops of terror in my veins and they grow cold in me, suddenly, and make me faint with fear because my heart and my imagination wander away from God into their own private idolatry. . . . I am exhausted by fear. (p. 248)

January 12, 1950

It is in deep solitude that I find the gentleness with which I can truly love my brothers. The more solitary

I am, the more affection I have for them. It is pure affection, and filled with reverence for the solitude of others. Solitude and silence teach me to love my brothers for what they are, not for what they say. (p. 261)

Solitude is not merely a negative relationship. It is not merely the absence of people. True solitude is a participation in the solitariness of God—Who is in all things. His solitude is not a local absence but a metaphysical transcendence. His solitude is His being. . . . those who cannot be alone cannot find their true being and they are always something less than themselves. . . . [For us] solitude means withdrawal from an artificial and fictional level of being which men, divided by original sin, have fabricated in order to keep peace with concupiscence and death. But by that very fact the solitary finds himself on the level of a more perfect spiritual society—the city of those who have become real enough to confess and glorify God (that is: life), in the teeth of death. (p. 262)

PART SIX: THE SIGN OF JONAS

November 19, 1950

Those who love God should attempt to preserve or create an atmosphere in which He can be found. Christians should have quiet homes. Throw out television, if necessary—not everybody, but those who take this sort of thing seriously. Radios useless. Stay away from the movies—I was going to say "as a penance" but it would seem to me to be rather a pleasure than a penance, to stay away from the movies. Maybe even form small agrarian communities in the country where there would be *no* radios, etc.

Let those who can stand a little silence find other people who like silence, and create silence and peace for one another. Bring up their kids not to yell so much. Children are naturally quiet—if they are left alone and not given the needle from the cradle upward, in order that they may develop into citizens of a state in which everybody yells and is yelled at. (pp. 301-02)

. . . When you gain this interior silence you can carry it around with you in the world, and pray everywhere. But just as interior asceticism cannot be acquired without concrete and exterior mortification, so it is absurd to talk about interior silence where there is no exterior silence. (p. 302)

December 13, 1950

There is nothing on this earth that does not give me a pain. Conversation in town, ambition in the cloister: I mean even ambition to do great things for God. That ambition is too much like the ambitions of the town.

I am aware of silence all around me in the country as of a world that is closed to men. They live in it and yet its door is closed to them. This silence, it is everywhere. It is the room Jesus told us to enter into when we pray. (p. 308)

March 3, 1951

How weary I am of being a writer. How necessary it is
for monks to work in the fields, in the rain, in the sun,
in the mud, in the clay, in the wind: these are our spiritual directors and our novice-masters. They form our
contemplation. They instill us with virtue. They make
us as stable as the land we live in. You do not get that
out of a typewriter. . . . (p. 311)

Coming to the monastery has been for me exactly the
right kind of withdrawal. It has given me perspective.
It has taught me how to live. And now I owe everyone
else in the world a share in that life. My first duty is to
start, for the first time, to live as a member of a human
race which is no more (and no less) ridiculous than I
am myself. And my first human act is the recognition of
how much I owe everybody else. (p. 312)

November 29, 1951

But once God has called you to solitude, everything you
touch leads you further into solitude. Everything that
affects you builds you into a hermit, as long as you do
not insist on doing the work yourself and building your
own kind of hermitage.

What is my new desert? The name of it is *compassion*. There is no wilderness so terrible, so beautiful, so
arid and so fruitful as the wilderness of compassion. It
is the only desert that shall truly flourish like the lily.
It shall become a pool, it shall bud forth and blossom

and rejoice with joy. It is in the desert of compassion that the thirsty land turns into springs of water, that the poor possess all things. (p. 323)

January 10, 1952

The more I get to know my scholastics the more reverence I have for their individuality and the more I meet them in my own solitude. The best of them, and the ones to whom I feel closest, are also the most solitary and at the same time the most charitable. All this experience replaces my theories of solitude. I do not need a hermitage, because I have found one where I least expected it. It was when I knew my brothers less well that my thoughts were more involved in them. Now that I know them better, I can see something of the depths of solitude which are in every human person, but which most men do not know how to lay open either to themselves or to others or to God. (p. 326)

March 17, 1952

When your tongue is silent, you can rest in the silence of the forest. When your imagination is silent, the forest speaks to you, tells you of its unreality and of the Reality of God. But when your mind is silent, then the forest suddenly becomes magnificently real and blazes transparently with the Reality of God: for now I know that the Creation which first seems to reveal Him, in concepts, then seems to hide Him, by the same concepts, finally *is revealed in Him,* in the Holy Spirit: and we who are in God find ourselves united, in Him, with all that springs from Him. This is prayer, and this is glory! (p. 332)

Epilogue: Fire Watch, July 4, 1952

God, my God, God Whom I meet in darkness, with You it is always the same thing! Always the same question that nobody knows how to answer!

I have prayed to You in the daytime with thoughts and reasons, and in the nighttime You have confronted me, scattering thought and reason. I have come to You in the morning with light and with desire, and You have descended upon me, with great gentleness, with most forbearing silence, in this inexplicable night, dispersing light, defeating all desire. I have explained to You a hundred times my motives for entering the monastery and You have listened and said nothing, and I have turned away and wept with shame.

Is it true that all my motives have meant nothing? Is it true that all my desires were an illusion?

While I am asking questions which You do not answer, You ask me a question which is so simple that I cannot answer. I do not even understand the question.

This night, and every night, it is the same question. (pp. 342-43)

I think . . . of all my . . . scholastics What is waiting to be born in all their hearts? Suffering? Deception? Heroism? Defeat? Peace? Betrayal? Sanctity? Death? Glory?

On all sides I am confronted by questions that I cannot answer, because the time for answering them has not yet come. Between the silence of God and the silence of my own soul, stands the silence of the souls entrusted to me. Immersed in these three silences, I realize that the questions I ask myself about them are perhaps no more than a surmise. And perhaps the most urgent and practical renunciation is the renunciation of all questions. (p. 344)

Lord God of this great night: do You see the woods? Do You hear the rumor of their loneliness? Do you behold their secrecy? Do You remember their solitudes? Do You see that my soul is beginning to dissolve like wax within me?

Clamabo per diem et non exaudies, et nocte et non ad insipientiam mihi! . . .

But there is greater comfort in the substance of silence than in the answer to a question. Eternity is in the present. Eternity is in the palm of the hand. Eternity is a seed of fire, whose sudden roots break barriers that keep my heart from being an abyss. . . .

. . . Questions arrive, assume their actuality, and also disappear. In this hour I shall cease to ask them, and silence shall be my answer. (pp. 350-51)

THOUGHTS IN SOLITUDE

When society is made up of men who know no interior solitude it can no longer be held together by love: and consequently it is held together by a violent and abusive authority. But when men are violently deprived of the solitude and freedom which are their due, the society in which they live becomes putrid, it festers with servility, resentment and hate. (p. 13)

This, then, is our desert: to live facing despair, but not to consent. To trample it down under hope in the Cross. (pp. 22-23)

For if our emotions really die in the desert, our humanity dies with them. We must return from the desert like Jesus or St. John, with our capacity for feeling expanded and deepened, strengthened against the appeals of falsity, warned against temptation, great, noble and pure. (p. 28)

Living is the constant adjustment of thought to life and life to thought in such a way that we are always growing, always experiencing new things in the old and old things in the new. Thus life is always new. (p. 30)

(The desire for virtue is frustrated in many men of good will by the distaste they instinctively feel for the false virtues of those who are supposed to be holy. Sinners have a very keen eye for false virtues and a very exacting idea of what virtue should be in a good man. If in the men who are supposed to be good they only see a "virtue" which is effectively less vital and less interesting than their own vices they will conclude that virtue

has no meaning, and will cling to what they have although they hate it.) (p. 32)

What is the use of praying if at the very moment of
prayer, we have so little confidence in God that we are
busy planning our own kind of answer to our prayer?
(p. 36)

We enjoy created things in hope. We enjoy them not as
they are in themselves but as they are in Christ—full
of promise. (p. 39)

In meditative prayer, one thinks and speaks not only
with his mind and lips, but in a certain sense with his
whole being. Prayer is then not just a formula of words,
or a series of desires springing up in the heart—it is the
orientation of our whole body, mind and spirit to God
in silence, attention, and adoration. All good meditative
prayer is a *conversion of our entire self to God.* (p. 48)

Poverty is the door to freedom . . . because, finding
nothing in ourselves that is a source of hope, we know
there is nothing in ourselves worth defending. There is
nothing special in ourselves to love. We go out of ourselves therefore and rest in Him in Whom alone is our
hope. (p. 53)

If you want to have a spiritual life you must unify your
life. A life is either all spiritual or not spiritual at all.
No man can serve two masters. (p. 55)

Often the poorest man in the community is the one who is at everybody else's disposition. He can be used by all and never takes time to do anything special for himself. (p. 58)

My life is a listening. His is a speaking. My salvation is to hear and respond. For this, my life must be silent. Hence, my silence is my salvation (p. 72)

. . . The beginning of wisdom is the confession of sin. This confession gains for us the mercy of God. It makes the light of His truth shine in our conscience, without which we cannot avoid sin. (p. 76)

A man becomes a solitary at the moment when, no matter what may be his external surroundings, he is suddenly aware of his own inalienable solitude and sees that he will never be anything but solitary. (p. 79)

My Lord God, I have no idea where I am going, I do not see the road ahead of me, I cannot know for certain where it will end. Nor do I really know myself, and the fact that I think I am following your will does not mean that I am actually doing so. But I believe that the desire to please you does in fact please you. And I hope I have that desire in all that I am doing. I hope that I will never do anything apart from that desire. And I know that if I do this you will lead me by the right road, though I may know nothing about it. Therefore I will trust you always though I may seem to be lost and in the shadow of death. I will not fear, for you are ever with me, and you will never leave me to face my perils alone. (p. 81)

Fundamentally, as Max Picard points out, it probably comes to this: living in a silence which so reconciles the contradictions within us that, although they remain within us, they cease to be a problem. (p. 82)

We put words between ourselves and things. Even God has become another conceptual unreality in a no-man's land of language that no longer serves as a means of communion with reality. (p. 83)

God . . . is found when He is sought and when He is no longer sought He escapes us. He is heard only when we hope to hear Him, and if, thinking our hope to be fulfilled, we cease to listen, He ceases to speak, His silence ceases to be vivid and becomes dead, even though we recharge it with the echo of our own emotional noise. (p. 86)

Let me seek, then, the gift of silence, and poverty, and solitude, where everything I touch is turned into prayer: where the sky is my prayer, the birds are my prayer, the wind in the trees is my prayer, for God is all in all. (p. 91)

It is a greater thing and a better prayer to live in Him Who is Infinite, and to rejoice that He is Infinite, than to strive always to press His infinity into the narrow space of our own hearts. (p. 94)

Do not flee to solitude from the community. Find God first in the community, then He will lead you to solitude. (p. 110)

CHAPTER 9

The Unmasking of an Illusion

LETTERS TO A WHITE LIBERAL
(FROM *SEEDS OF DESTRUCTION*)

Introductory Note

Why . . . is there so much hatred and so dreadful a
need for explosive violence? Because of the impotency
and the frustration of a society that sees itself involved
in difficulties which, though this may not consciously
be admitted, promise to be insuperable. Actually, there
is no reason why they *should* be insuperable, but as
long as white society persists in clinging to its present
condition and to its own image of itself as the only ac-
ceptable reality, then the problem will remain without
reasonable solution, and there will inevitably be violence.

The problem is this: If the Negro . . . enters wholly into white society, then *that society is going to be radically changed.* (p. 16)

Letter I

. . . We are bound to search "history," that is to say the intelligible actions of men, for some indications of their inner significance, and *some relevance to our commitment as Christians.* (p. 18)

It was only when money became involved that the Negro demonstrations finally impressed themselves upon the American mind as being real.

We claim to judge reality by the touchstone of Christian values, such as freedom, reason, the spirit, faith, personalism, etc. In actual fact we judge them by commercial values: sales, money, price, profits. It is not the life of the spirit that is real to us, but the vitality of the *market.* Spiritual values are to us, in actual fact, meaningless unless they can be reduced to terms of buying and selling. . . .

Thus we end up by treating persons as objects for sale, and therefore as meaningless unless they have some value on the market. A man is to us nothing more nor less than "what he is worth." (p. 27)

Letter II

Now, my liberal friend, here is your situation. You, the well-meaning liberal, are right in the middle of all this confusion. . . . On the one hand, with your good will and your ideals, your fine hopes and your generous, but vague, love of mankind in the abstract and of rights enthroned on a juridical Olympus, you offer a certain encouragement to the Negro . . . so that, abetted by you, he is emboldened to demand concessions. Though he knows you will not support all his demands, he is well aware that you will be forced to support some of them in order to maintain your image of yourself as a liberal. He also knows, however, that your material comforts, your security, and your congenial relations with the establishment are much more important to you than your rather volatile idealism, and that when the game gets rough you will be quick to see your own interests menaced by his demands. And you will sell him down the river for the five hundredth time in order to protect yourself. For this reason, as well as to support your own self-esteem, you are very anxious to have a position of leadership and control in the Negro's fight for rights, in order to be able to apply the brakes when you feel it is necessary. (p. 33)

. . . You will prefer your own security to everything else, and you will be willing to sacrifice the Negro to preserve yourself.

But it is precisely in this that you are contributing to the inexorable development of a revolution, for revolutions are always the result of situations in which the drive of an underprivileged mass of men can no longer be contained by token concessions, and in which the establishment is too confused, too inert and too frightened to *participate* with the underprivileged in a new and creative solution of what is realized to be *their common problem.* (p. 36)

At the end of this chain of thought I visualize you, my liberal friend, goose-stepping down Massachusetts Avenue in the uniform of an American Totalitarian Party in a mass rally where nothing but the most uproarious approval is manifest, except, by implication, on the part of silent and strangely scented clouds of smoke drifting over from the new "camps" where the "Negroes are living in retirement." (p. 38)

Letter III

. . . The struggle for liberty is not merely regarded by this most significant sector of the Negro population as a fight for political rights. It is this, and it is also much more. It is what Gandhi called *satyagrāha*—a struggle first of all for the *truth,* outside and independent of specific political contingencies.

The mystique of Negro nonviolence holds that the victory of truth is inevitable, but that the redemption of individuals is not inevitable. Though the truth will win, since in Christ it has already conquered, not everyone can "come to the light"—for if his works are darkness, he fears to let them be seen. (p. 39)

The purpose of nonviolent protest, in its deepest and most spiritual dimensions is then to awaken the conscience of the white man to the awful reality of his injustice and of his sin, so that he will be able to see that the Negro problem is really a *white* problem: that the cancer of injustice and hate which is eating white society and is only partly manifested in racial segregation with all its consequences, *is rooted in the heart of the white man himself.* (pp. 40-41)

If they are forced to listen to what the Negro is trying to say, the whites may have to admit that *their prosperity is rooted to some extent in injustice and in sin.* And, in consequence, this might lead to a complete reexamination of the political motives behind all our current policies, domestic and foreign, with the possible admission that we are wrong. Such an admission might, in fact, be so disastrous that its effects would dislocate our whole economy and ruin the country. These are not things that are consciously admitted, but they are confusedly present in our minds. They account for the passionate and mindless desperation with which we plunge this way and that, trying to evade the implications of our present crisis. (p. 42)

. . . The irony is that the Negro . . . *is offering the white man a "message of salvation," but the white man is so blinded by his self-sufficiency and self-conceit that he does not recognize the peril in which he puts himself by ignoring the offer.* (p. 52)

. . . The Negro, in fact, has nothing to sell. He is only offering us the occasion *to enter with him into a providential reciprocity willed for us by God.* He is inviting us to understand him as necessary to our own lives, and as completing them. He is warning us that we cannot do without him, and that if we insist on regarding him as an enemy, an object of contempt, or a rival, we will perhaps sterilize and ruin our own lives. He is telling us that unless we can enter into a vital and Christian relationship with him, there will be hate, violence and civil war indeed: and from this violence perhaps none of us will emerge whole. (pp. 52-53)

The Legend of Tucker Caliban

One finds everywhere in American Negro society a more or less explicit anticipation of the end of the white domination of the world and the decline of European-American civilization. The Negro therefore cannot be content merely to be integrated into something he regards as already over and done with. . . . (p. 61)

. . . The hour of freedom is seen also as an hour of salvation. But it is not an hour of salvation for the Negro only. The white man, if he can possibly open the ears of his heart and listen intently enough to hear what the Negro is now hearing, can recognize that he is himself called to freedom and to salvation in the same *kairos* of events which he is now, in so many different ways, opposing or resisting. (p. 65)

The real tragedy is that of the white man who does not realize that though he seems to himself to be free, he is actually the victim of the same servitudes which he has imposed on the Negro: passive subjection to the lotus-eating commercial society that he has tried to create for himself, and which is shot through with falsity and unfreedom from top to bottom. He makes a great deal of fuss about "individual freedom," but one may ask if such freedom really exists. Is there really a genuine freedom for the person or only the irresponsibility of the atomized individual members of mass society? (pp. 66-67)

The white man is so far gone that he cannot free the Negro because he cannot even free himself. Hence these books [of James Baldwin and William Melvin Kelley] are not in any sense demanding that the whites now finally free the Negroes. On the contrary, the magnificent paradox they utter is that the Negro has a mission to free the white man: and he can begin to do this if he learns to free himself. His first step to freedom must be the clear realization that he cannot depend on the white man or trust him for anything, since the white man is hopelessly impotent, deluded and stupefied by his own alienation. (p. 69)

THE HOT SUMMER OF SIXTY-SEVEN
(FROM *FAITH AND VIOLENCE*)

To sum it up: the problem as I see it is this. The Negro has in some sense abandoned the struggle for Civil Rights. He has given up Christian nonviolence as futile idealism. He has decided that whitey only understands one kind of language: violence. The Negro has con-

cluded that if whitey wants to terrorize Vietnamese
with napalm and other cozy instruments of war, he
should have a little taste of what fire and terror feel
like at home. So in effect the Negro is declaring guerilla
war on white society. . . .

Now the Negro knows, or should know, that he cannot really win this kind of civil war. But he can become
so provocative as to dislocate this highly organized
technological system of ours. If President Johnson con-
tinues trying to pull the country together by getting
it more and more involved in fighting an outside enemy (Asians) and if the country gets mixed up in a
war with China, and if the Negro then decides it is
a good time to shake the foundations here at home . . .
I need not elaborate on the picture. It could be catas-
trophic. (p. 175)

The most likely thing is that extreme provocation by
irrational violence may create such disorder and such
panic in the country that a new order based on force
(a police state) may have to be established. In that
event, the possibility of extremists on the white side
taking over and ruling by irrational and arbitrary violence is very likely. Even "prison camps" for Negroes
and then for other unacceptables are not beyond the
bounds of possibility. At times one feels that the Negroes are unconsciously willing to provoke this. (p. 176)

I do not think any form of white extremism will be an
adequate answer. And I do hope that we will keep our
heads enough to prevent a complete polarization, a split

which makes all reasonable communication between the races impossible. We must continue to treat our Negro friends as persons and as friends, not as members of a hostile and incomprehensible species, and it is to be hoped that they will do us the same honor. . . .

As Christians, we must remember that in Christ there is no meaning to racial divisions. There is no white and black in Christ: but if Christianity is being discredited in the eyes of Negroes, that does not dispense us from our duty to be authentic Christians toward the Negro whether he likes us or not. It is not our job to convince him that Christianity is "true" or "genuine," but to live up to what we ourselves profess to believe, so that we may not be judged by God for a mere lip-service that has (as we now begin to realize too late) reached the proportions of worldwide scandal. (p. 179)

A TRIBUTE TO GANDHI
(FROM *SEEDS OF DESTRUCTION*)

What is certainly true is that Gandhi not only understood the ethic of the Gospel as well, if not in some ways better, than many Christians, but he is one of the very few men of our time who applied Gospel principles to the problems of a political and social existence in such a way that his approach to these problems was *inseparably* religious and political at the same time (p. 159)

. . . Political action . . . was not a means to acquire security and strength for one's self and one's party, but

a means of witnessing to the truth and the reality of
the cosmic structure by making one's own proper contribution to the order willed by God. One could thus
preserve one's integrity and peace, being detached from
results (which are in the hands of God) and being
free from the inner violence that comes from division
and untruth. . . .

The success with which Gandhi applied this spiritual
force to political action makes him uniquely important
in our age. . . . (p. 160)

. . . The radical difference between him and other leaders, even the most sincere and honest of them, becomes
evident by the fact that Gandhi is chiefly concerned
with truth and with service, *svadharma,* rather than
with the possible success of his tactics upon other people, and paradoxically it was his religious conviction
that made Gandhi a great politician rather than a mere
tactician or operator. (p. 161)

. . . Gandhi recognized, as no other world leader of our
time has done, the necessity to be free from the pres-
sures, the exorbitant and tyrannical demands of a society
that is violent because it is essentially greedy, lustful
and cruel. Therefore he fasted, observed days of silence,
lived frequently in retreat, knew the value of solitude,
as well as of the totally generous expenditure of his
time and energy in listening to others and communicating with them. He recognized the impossibility of
being a peaceful and nonviolent man if one submits
passively to the insatiable requirements of a society

maddened by overstimulation and obsessed with the demons of noise, voyeurism and speed.

"Jesus died in vain," said Gandhi, "if he did not teach us to regulate the whole of life by the eternal law of love." (p. 163)

Gandhi believed that the central problem of our time was the acceptance or the rejection of a basic law of love and truth which had been made known to the world in traditional religions and most clearly by Jesus Christ. Gandhi himself expressly and very clearly declared himself an adherent of this one law. His whole life, his political action, finally even his death, were nothing but a witness to his commitment. *"If love is not the law of our being the whole of my argument falls to pieces."* (p. 164)

GANDHI AND THE ONE-EYED GIANT
(FROM *GANDHI ON NONVIOLENCE*)

It was the spiritual consciousness of a people that awakened in the spirit of one person. But the message of the Indian spirit, of Indian wisdom, was not for India alone. It was for the entire world. Hence Gandhi's message was valid for India and for himself in so far as it represented *the awakening of a new world.* (p. 5)

. . . The spirit of nonviolence sprang from *an inner realization of spiritual unity in himself.* The whole Gandhian concept of nonviolent action and *satyagraha* [holding on to truth] is incomprehensible if it is thought to be a

means of achieving unity rather than as *the fruit of
inner unity already achieved. . . .*

The first thing of all and the most important of all
was the inner unity, the overcoming and healing of
inner division, the consequent spiritual and personal
freedom, of which national autonomy and liberty would
only be consequences. (p. 6)

The spiritual life of one person is simply the life of all
manifesting itself in him. While it is very necessary to
emphasize the truth that as the person deepens his own
thought in silence he enters into a deeper understanding of and communion with the spirit of his entire people . . ., it is also important to remember that as he becomes engaged in the crucial struggles of his people, in
seeking justice and truth together with his brother, he
tends to liberate the truth in himself by seeking true
liberty for all. (p. 6)

. . . Even his days of silence and retirement were not
days of mere "privacy"; they belonged to India and he
owed them to India, because his "spiritual life" was
simply his participation in the life and *dharma* of his
people. Their liberation and the recovery of their political unity would be meaningless unless their liberty
and unity had a dimension that was primarily spiritual
and religious. (p. 7)

It is not possible for the truly nonviolent man simply
to ignore the inherent falsity and inner contradictions

of a violent society. On the contrary, it is for him a religious and human duty to confront the untruth in that
society with his own witness in order that the falsity
may become evident to everyone. The first job of a
satyagrahi [someone who holds onto the truth] is to
bring the real situation to light even if he has to suffer
and die in order that injustice be unmasked and appear
for what it really is. (p. 10)

[Society] is always "in becoming." It is on the loom,
and it is made up of constantly changing relationships.
Nonviolence takes account precisely of this dynamic
and nonfinal state of all relationships among men, for
nonviolence seeks to change relationships that are evil
into others that are good, or at least less bad.

Hence nonviolence implies a kind of bravery far different from violence. In the use of force, one simplifies
the situation by assuming that the evil to be overcome
is clear-cut, definite, and irreversible. Hence there remains but one thing: to eliminate it. Any dialogue with
the sinner, any question of the irreversibility of his act,
only means faltering and failure. Failure to eliminate
evil is itself a defeat. . . .

The greatest of tyrannies are all therefore based on
the postulate that *there should never be any sin*. (pp.
13-14)

A violent change would not have been a serious change
at all. To punish and destroy the oppressor is merely
to initiate a new cycle of violence and oppression. The

only real liberation is that which *liberates both the oppressor and the oppressed* at the same time from the same tyrannical automatism of the violent process which contains in itself the curse of irreversibility. . . .

True freedom is then inseparable from the inner strength which can assume the common burden of evil which weighs both on oneself and one's adversary. False freedom is only a manifestation of the weakness that cannot bear even one's own evil until it is projected onto the other and seen as exclusively his. The highest form of spiritual freedom is, as Gandhi believed, to be sought in the strength of heart which is capable of liberating the oppressed and the oppressor together. But in any event, the oppressed must be able to be free within himself, so that he may begin to gain strength to pity his oppressor. (pp. 14-15)

CHAPTER 10

Discovery of the East

THE WAY OF CHUANG TZU

. . . I have enjoyed writing this book more than any other I can remember. . . .

I simply like Chuang Tzu because he is what he is and I feel no need to justify this liking to myself or to anyone else. He is far too great to need any apologies from me. If St. Augustine could read Plotinus, if St. Thomas could read Aristotle and Averroes (both of them certainly a long way further from Christianity than Chuang Tzu ever was!), and if Teilhard de Chardin could make copious use of Marx and Engels in his synthesis, I think I may be pardoned for consorting with a Chinese recluse who shares the climate and peace of my own kind of solitude, and who is my own kind of person. (pp. 9-11)

[Chuang Tzu] believes that the whole concept of "happiness" and "unhappiness" is ambiguous from the start, since it is situated in the world of objects. This is no less true of more refined concepts like virtue, justice, and so on. In fact, it is especially true of "good and evil," or "right and wrong." From the moment they are treated as "objects to be attained," these values lead to delusion and alienation. Therefore Chuang Tzu agrees with the paradox of Lao Tzu, "When all the world recognizes good as good, it becomes evil," because it becomes something that one does not have and which one must constantly be pursuing until, in effect, it becomes unattainable. (p. 23)

The more one seeks "the good" outside oneself as something to be acquired, the more one is faced with the necessity of discussing, studying, understanding, analyzing the nature of the good. The more, therefore, one becomes involved in abstractions and in the confusion of divergent opinions. The more "the good" is objectively analyzed, the more it is treated as something to be attained by special virtuous techniques, the less real it becomes. As it becomes less real, it recedes further into the distance of abstraction, futurity, unattainability. The more, therefore, one concentrates on the means to be used to attain it. And as the end becomes more remote and more difficult, the means become more elaborate and complex, until finally the mere study of the means becomes so demanding that all one's effort must be concentrated on this, and the end is forgotten. . . . This is, in fact, nothing but organized despair: "the good" that is preached and exacted by the moralist thus finally becomes an evil, and all the more so since the hopeless pursuit of it distracts one from the real good which one already possesses and which one now despises or ignores. (p. 23)

The secret of the way proposed by Chuang Tzu is . . . not the accumulation of virtue and merit . . . but . . . the non-doing, or non-action, which is not intent upon results and is not concerned with consciously laid plans or deliberately organized endeavors: "My greatest happiness consists precisely in doing nothing whatever that is calculated to obtain happiness . . . Perfect joy is to be without joy . . . if you ask 'what ought to be done' and 'what ought not to be done' on earth to produce happiness, I answer that these questions do not have [a fixed and predetermined] answer" to suit every case. If one is in harmony with Tao—the cosmic Tao, "Great Tao"—the answer will make itself clear when the time comes to act, for then one will act not according to the human and self-conscious mode of deliberation, but according to the divine and spontaneous mode of wu wei, which is the mode of action of Tao itself, and is therefore the source of all good. (p. 24)

For Chuang Tzu, the truly great man is therefore not the man who has, by a lifetime of study and practice, accumulated a great fund of virtue and merit, but the man in whom "Tao acts without impediment," the "man of Tao." (p. 25)

A contemplative and interior life which would simply make the subject more aware of himself and permit him to become obsessed with his own interior progress

would, for Chuang Tzu, be no less an illusion than the
active life of the "benevolent" man who would try by
his own efforts to impose his idea of the good on those
who might oppose this idea—and thus in his eyes, become "enemies of the good." The true tranquillity
sought by the "man of Tao" is *Ying ning*, tranquillity in
the action of non-action, in other words, a tranquillity
which transcends the division between activity and
contemplation by entering into union with the nameless
and invisible Tao. (p. 26)

The key to Chuang Tzu's thought is the complimen-
tarity of opposites, and this can be seen only when one
grasps the central "pivot" of Tao which passes squarely
through both "Yes" and "No," "I" and "Not-I." Life is a
continual development. All beings are in a state of flux.
Chuang Tzu would have agreed with Herakleitos. What
is impossible today may suddenly become possible tomorrow. What is good and pleasant today may, tomorrow, become evil and odious. What seems right from
one point of view may, when seen from a different aspect, manifest itself as completely wrong. (p. 30)

ZEN AND THE BIRDS OF APPETITE

1. The Study of Zen

. . . In the words of D. T. Suzuki, Zen is "beyond the
world of opposites, a world built up by intellectual distinction . . . a spiritual world of nondistinction which
involves achieving an absolute point of view. . . . The

Absolute is in no way distinct from the world of discrimination. . . The Absolute is in the world of opposites and not apart from it." (pp. 3-4)

[If we see Meister Eckhart] in relation to those Zen
Masters on the other side of the earth who, like him,
deliberately used extremely paradoxical expressions, we
can detect in him the same kind of consciousness as
theirs. Whatever Zen may be, however you define it, it is
somehow there in Eckhart. But the way to see it is not
first to define Zen and then apply the definition both to
him and to the Japanese Zen Masters. The real way to
study Zen is to penetrate the outer shell and taste the
inner kernel which cannot be defined. Then one realizes
in oneself the reality which is being talked about. (p 13)

2. New Consciousness

. . . The developing Christian consciousness is one
which is activistic, antimystical, antimetaphysical, which
eschews well-defined and concrete forms, and which
tends to identify itself with active, progressive, even
revolutionary, movements that are on the way but that
have not yet reached any kind of clear definition.

In this context, then, the concept of the self as a very
present, very concrete center of decision has considerable importance. It matters very much what you are
thinking, saying, doing, deciding, here and now. It
matters very much what your current commitments are,
whom you are with, whom you are against, where you
claim to be going, what button you wear, whom you

vote for—all this is important. This is obviously proper
to men of action who feel that there are old structures
to be torn down and new ones to be built. But from
such men we must not yet expect either patience with
or understanding of mysticism. They will be fore-
doomed, by their very type of consciousness, to reject
it as irrelevant and even un-Christian. Meanwhile we
may wonder if what they are developing is not simply
a new, more fluid, less doctrinal kind of conformism!
(p. 29)

3. A Christian Looks at Zen

But the chief characteristic of Zen is that it rejects all
these systematic elaborations in order to get back, as
far as possible, to the pure unarticulated and unex-
plained ground of direct experience. The direct experience of what? Life itself. What it means that I exist,
that I live: who is this "I" that exists and lives? What
is the difference between an authentic and an illusory
awareness of the self that exists and lives? What are
and are not the basic facts of existence? . . .

The whole aim of Zen is not to make foolproof statements about experience, but to come to direct grips
with reality without the mediation of logical verbal-
izing. . . .

The Zen experience is a direct grasp of the *unity* of
the invisible and the visible, the noumenal and the
phenomenal, or, if you prefer, an experiential realization that any such division is bound to be pure imagination. (pp. 36-37)

Now the great obstacle to mutual understanding between Christianity and Buddhism lies in the Western tendency to focus not on the Buddhist *experience,* which is essential, but on the *explanation,* which is accidental and which indeed Zen often regards as completely trivial and even misleading. (pp. 37-38)

Is it therefore possible to say that both Christians and Buddhists can equally well practice Zen? Yes, if by Zen we mean precisely the quest for direct and pure experience on a metaphysical level, liberated from verbal formulas and linguistic preconceptions. On the theological level the question becomes more complex. ... (p. 44)

Now in Zen, what is communicated is not a message. ... It is not a "what." It does not bring "news" which the receiver did not already have, about something the one informed did not yet know. What Zen communicates is an awareness that is potentially already there but is not conscious of itself. Zen is then not Kerygma but realization, not revelation but consciousness, not news from the Father who sends His Son into this world, but awareness of the ontological ground of our own being here and now, right in the midst of the world. (p. 47)

"Zen teaches nothing; it merely enables us to wake up and become aware. It does not teach, it points." (Suzuki, *Introduction,* p. 38) The acts and gestures of a Zen Master are no more "statements" than is the ringing of an alarm clock. (pp. 49-50)

4. Transcendent Experience

... It is basic to Zen ... and to Christian mysticism ...
*to radically and unconditionally question the ego which
appears to be the subject of the transcendent experience,* and thus of course to radically question the whole
nature of the experience itself precisely as "experience."
Are we any longer able to speak of an experience when
the subject of the experience is not a limited, well-
defined, empirical subject? Or, to put it in other words,
are we able to speak of "consciousness" when the conscious subject is no longer able to be aware of itself as
separate and unique? Then if the empirical ego is conscious at all, is it conscious of itself as transcended, left
behind, irrelevant, illusory, and indeed as the root of all
ignorance (*avidya*)? ...

In the Christian tradition the focus of this "experience" is found not in the individual self as a separate,
limited and temporal ego, but in Christ, or the Holy
Spirit "within" this self. In Zen it is Self with a capital S,
that is to say precisely *not* the ego-self. This Self is the
Void. (pp. 73-74)

More specifically, all transcendent experience is for the
Christian a participation in "the mind of Christ"—"Let
this mind be in you which was also in Christ Jesus ...
who emptied himself . . . obedient unto death. . . .
Therefore God raised him and conferred upon him a
name above all names." (Phil 2:5-10) This dynamic of
emptying and of transcendence accurately defines the

transformation of the Christian consciousness in Christ. It is a kenotic transformation, an emptying of all the contents of the ego-consciousness to become a void in which the light of God or the glory of God, the full radiation of the infinite reality of His Being and Love are manifested. (p. 75)

Note that in Buddhism also the highest development of consciousness is that by which the individual ego is completely emptied and becomes identified with the enlightened Buddha, or rather finds itself to be in reality the enlightened Buddha mind. Nirvana is not the consciousness of an ego that is aware of itself as having crossed over to "the other shore" (to be on "another shore" is the same as not having crossed over), but the Absolute Ground-Consciousness of the Void, in which there are no shores. Thus the Buddhist enters into the self-emptying and enlightenment of Buddha as the Christian enters into the self-emptying (crucifixion) and glorification (resurrection and ascension) of Christ. The chief difference between the two is that the former is existential and ontological, the latter is theological and personal. But "person" here must be distinguished from "the individual empirical ego." (p. 76)

Hence it becomes overwhelmingly important for us *to become detached from our everyday conception of ourselves as potential subjects for special and unique experiences, or as candidates for realization, attainment and fulfillment.* In other words, this means that a spiritual guide worth his salt will conduct a ruthless campaign against all forms of delusion arising out of spiritual ambition and self-complacency which aim to establish the ego in spiritual glory. That is why a St. John of the Cross is so hostile to visions, ecstasies and all forms of "special experience." That is why the Zen Masters say: "If you meet the Buddha, kill him." (pp. 76-77)

5. *Postface*

To exist and function in the world of opposites while experiencing that world in terms of a primal simplicity does imply if not a formal metaphysic, at least a ground of metaphysical intuition. This means a totally different perspective than that which dominates our society— and enables it to dominate us.

Hence the Zen saying: before I grasped Zen, the mountains were nothing but mountains and the rivers nothing but rivers. When I got into Zen, the mountains were no longer mountains and the rivers no longer rivers. But when I understood Zen, the mountains were only mountains and the rivers only rivers. (p. 140)

The thing about Zen is that it pushes contradictions to their ultimate limit where one has to choose between madness and innocence. And Zen suggests that we may be driving toward one or the other on a cosmic scale. . . . (p. 141)

Bibliography

I. *Books by Thomas Merton*

1. *Thirty Poems.* New York: New Directions, 1944
2. *A Man in the Divided Sea.* New York: New Directions, 1946.
3. *Figures for an Apocalypse.* New York: New Directions, 1948.
4. *Cistercian Contemplatives.* New York: Marbridge Printing Co., Inc., 1948.
5. *The Seven Storey Mountain.* New York: Harcourt, Brace and Co., 1948. (New American Library Paperback, 1963).
6. *What is Contemplation?* Holy Cross, Ind.: St. Mary's College Press, 1948.
7. *Exile Ends in Glory.* Milwaukee: The Bruce Publishing Company, 1948.
8. *Seeds of Contemplation.* New York: New Directions, 1949.

9. *The Waters of Siloe.* New York: Harcourt, Brace and Co., Inc., 1949. (Doubleday Image, 1962).

10. *The Tears of the Blind Lions.* New York: New Directions, 1949.

11 *What Are These Wounds?* Milwaukee: The Bruce Publishing Co., 1950.

12. *The Ascent to Truth.* New York: Harcourt, Brace and Co., 1951. (Viking Compass, 1959).

13. *A Balanced Life of Prayer.* Trappist, Ky.: Abbey of Gethsemani, 1951.

14. *The Sign of Jonas.* New York: Harcourt, Brace and Co., 1953. (Doubleday Image, 1956).

15. *Bread in the Wilderness.* New York: New Directions, 1953.

16. *The Last of the Fathers.* New York: Harcourt, Brace and Co., 1954.

17. *No Man Is An Island.* New York: Harcourt, Brace and Co., 1955. (Doubleday Image, 1967).

18. *The Living Bread.* New York: Farrar, Straus and Cudahy, 1956.

19. *Silence in Heaven.* New York: Studio Publications and Thomas Y. Crowell, 1956.

20. *The Strange Islands.* New York: New Dimensions, 1957.

21. *The Tower of Babel.* New York: New Directions, 1957.

22. *The Silent Life.* New York: Farrar, Straus, 1957. (Dell, 1959).

23. *Thoughts in Solitude.* New York: Farrar, Straus and Cudahy, 1958.

24. *Monastic Peace.* Saint Paul, Minn.: North Central Publishing Co., 1958.

25. *The Secular Journal of Thomas Merton.* New York: Farrar, Straus, 1959. (Dell, 1960).

26. *Selected Poems of Thomas Merton.* New York: New Directions, 1959. (Enlarged edition, 1967).
27. *The Wisdom of the Desert.* New York: New Directions, 1960.
28. *Disputed Questions.* New York: Farrar, Straus, 1960. (New American Library, 1965).
29. *The Behavior of Titans.* New York: New Directions, 1961.
30. *New Seeds of Contemplation.* New York: New Directions, 1961.
31. *The New Man.* New York: Farrar, Straus, 1961. (New American Library, 1963).
32. *A Thomas Merton Reader.* Edited by Thomas P. McDonnell. New York: Harcourt, Brace and World, Inc., 1962.
33. *Original Child Bomb.* New York: New Directions, 1962.
34. *Breakthrough to Peace.* New York: New Directions, 1962.
35. *Life and Holiness.* New York: Herder and Herder, 1963. (Doubleday Image, 1964).
36. *Emblems of a Season of Fury.* New York: New Directions, 1963.
37. *Seeds of Destruction.* New York: Farrar Straus and Cudahy, 1964. (Macmillan, 1967).
38. *The Way of Chuang Tzu.* New York: New Directions, 1965.
39. *Gandhi on Non-Violence.* New York: New Directions, 1965.
40. *Seasons of Celebration.* New York: Farrar, Straus and Giroux, 1965.
41. *Raid on the Unspeakable.* New York: New Directions, 1966.

42. *Conjectures of a Guilty Bystander.* Garden City, N. Y.: Doubleday and Co., Inc., 1966.
43. *Redeeming the Time.* London: Burns and Oates Limited, 1966.
44. *Mystics and Zen Masters.* New York: Straus and Giroux, 1967. (Delta, 1969).
45. *Cables to the Ace.* New York: New Directions, 1968.
46. *Faith and Violence.* South Bend, Ind.: University of Notre Dame Press, 1968.
47. *Zen and the Birds of Appetite.* New York: New Directions, 1968.
48. *The Plague.* Religious Dimensions in Literature. The Seabury Reading Program. RDL$_7$. Lee A. Belford, general editor. New York: The Seabury Press, 1968.
49. *Contemplative Prayer.* New York: Herder and Herder, 1969.
50. *The Geography of Lograire.* New York: New Directions, 1969.
51. *My Argument with the Gestapo.* Garden City, N.Y.: Doubleday and Company, Inc., 1969.
52. *The True Solitude: A Selected Merton.* New York: Hallmark, 1969.
53. *Contemplation in a World of Action.* New York: Saturday Review Press, 1971.
54. *Thomas Merton on Peace.* Edited by Gordon Zahn. New York: Saturday Review Press, 1971.
55. *Asian Journal.* New York: New Directions, 1972.

II. *Books about Thomas Merton*

1. Baker, James Thomas, *Thomas Merton Social Critic.* Lexington: University of Kentucky Press, 1971.

2. Griffin, John Howard, *Hidden Wholeness: The Visual World of Thomas Merton.* Boston: Houghton Mifflin, 1970.
3. Griffin, et al., *Thomas Merton Studies Center,* Vol. 1, Santa Barbara: Unicorn Press, 1971.
4. Higgins, John J., *Merton's Theology of Prayer.* Spencer, Mass.: Cistercian Publications, 1972.
5. Rice, Edward, *The Man in the Sycamore Tree: The Good Times and Hard Life of Thomas Merton.* New York: Doubleday, 1971. (Doubleday Image, 1972).
6. Zahn, Gordon, editor and introduction, *Thomas Merton on Peace.* New York: Saturday Review Press, 1971.